CONTENTS

NOTICE

MOBILIZING A DOMINION

"Newfoundland entered the war as complete an example of unpreparedness and pacifism as could be found in the world. There was no military organization, no militia, no military machinery of any kind, and no trained experts on the spot to create it."

—*Patrick Thomas McGrath, journalist, politician, and member of the Newfoundland Patriotic Association*

ON THE EVE OF WAR

Newfoundland and Labrador was not ready for war in 1914. It did not have an army and its government did not have a military department. British troops once guarded the island, but that changed in 1870 when London withdrew its garrison. The Newfoundland government did not have the will or money to create a militia of its own and remained largely unconcerned with defence for the next 44 years.

By 1914, the closest things the dominion had to ground troops were a 100-man police force (half of the men served in St. John's and the others were scattered across the island) and five paramilitary groups. Four were church-sponsored youth brigades: the Anglican Church Lads' Brigade (CLB),

Pre-War Newfoundland and Labrador

What is today the Canadian province of Newfoundland and Labrador was in 1914 a self-governing dominion of the British Empire. Its official title was Newfoundland, even though its borders included the mainland territory of Labrador. The dominion's revenue was modest, about $3.5 million per year, and its largest industry was the cod fishery.

Most of its 250,000 inhabitants were fishers who lived in small and often isolated coastal settlements known as outports. About 32,000 lived in St. John's, which was Newfoundland's commercial and political centre. Employment was more diverse in the city, where many people worked in offices, shops, factories, schools, and workshops. Two other places had also diversified away from the fishery—the mining town of Wabana on Bell Island and the pulp and paper towns of Grand Falls and Bishop's Falls in central Newfoundland.

The Church Lads' Brigade Brass Band, 1904.
Archives and Special Collections (ASC), Coll. 137 04.02.009

the Catholic Cadet Corps, the Methodist Guards, and the Presbyterian Church's Newfoundland Highlanders.

Most cadets were teenagers, although some corps accepted men in their 20s. The brigades' goals were to improve the physical fitness and leadership skills of its members and to teach Christian ethics and values. Although cadets wore military-style uniforms and practiced marching, they were in no way ready to go to war.

The fifth paramilitary group was the Legion of Frontiersmen. It was a non-denominational organization for adult men that had formed in the United Kingdom in 1905 and then spread across the British Empire. By 1914, there were about 150 Frontiersmen in Newfoundland and Lab-

rador. Most of its branches were in Labrador—at Nain, Mud Lake, Battle Harbour, Grand River, and Red Bay—but there were also members on the island, at St. Anthony and St. John's. The Frontiersmen practiced marching and marksmanship, but its members had to supply their own guns.

The dominion's maritime defences were a little more promising than its land forces. A local branch of the Royal Naval Reserve had formed at St. John's in 1900 to provide a pool of recruits for Britain's Royal Navy in the event of war. Reservists spent 28 days in training each year. They learned how to use rifles and heavy guns and how to serve aboard ships of the Royal Navy. By 1914, there were about 600 reservists in Newfoundland and Labrador; almost all were

The Leaders in 1914

Sir Edward Morris

Prime minister and leader of the People's Party.

The People's Party was strongest in southern Newfoundland and the Avalon Peninsula. It was supported by Roman Catholic voters and the powerful Water Street merchants. In the 1913 general election, the People's Party had won 21 of the House of Assembly's 36 seats.

William Coaker

Leader of the Union Party and the Fishermen's Protective Union.

Coaker was a rising star in Newfoundland politics. Eight of the Union Party's nine candidates had won seats in the 1913 general election, including Coaker in Bonavista Bay. The ninth candidate had lost by a scant nine votes. The Union Party represented working-class interests and was strongest in Protestant outport districts on Newfoundland's northeast coast. Its popularity was spreading and, in 1914, many people believed it would win the next general election.

James Kent

Leader of the Liberal Party and of the combined Liberal-Union Opposition.

The Liberal Party had won fewer seats than the Union Party in the 1913 election, but its members had much more political experience. For that reason, Coaker allowed Kent to lead their combined Opposition in the House of Assembly.

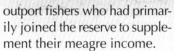

outport fishers who had primarily joined the reserve to supplement their meagre income.

Newfoundland was not just militarily unprepared for war in 1914. Its struggling economy and unpopular government also undermined the dominion's ability to launch an effective war effort.

Sir Edward Morris was Newfoundland's prime minister. His People's Party had been re-elected to the House of Assembly in 1913, but its majority had dropped from 10 seats to five and many of its candidates had only been elected by a slim majority of votes. The People's Party had lost important districts to the newly formed Union Party, which partnered with the Liberal Party to form a combined Opposition in the House of Assembly. Together, the Union and Liberal parties had won the popular vote.

Morris was in a weak political position and his popularity continued to fall after the election. If he was to orchestrate an effective war effort that would not ruin his political career, he would need the support of both the Liberal and Union parties. He would also need the back-ing of key public figures—most notably the leaders of the Anglican, Roman Catholic, and Methodist Churches. Securing their unified support would be no small feat in a society deeply and historically divided along religious lines.

Making matters even worse, Newfoundland and Labrador had entered an economic downturn shortly before the war began. Its largest industry was the centuries-old cod-fishery, but it was struggling. Increased competition from Norwegian and French fishers had cut deeply into profits and siphoned off important buyers in the Mediterranean. By 1914, Newfoundland's traditional European markets had been largely replaced by less-profitable ones in the Caribbean and Brazil.

The dominion suffered a series of deficits and entered the war with a national debt of $30.5 million—a heavy burden for a small and overwhelmingly poor population.

It was in this atmosphere of military unpreparedness, economic hardship, and political turmoil that Newfoundland and Labrador entered World War I.

Walter Frederic Rendell, wearing the uniform of the Legion of Frontiersmen, 1914. *The Rooms Provincial Archives Division, VA 36-33.7*

5

Follow me!

YOUR COUNTRY NEEDS YOU

War in Europe

At the start of the 20th century, Europe was divided. Its major powers had splintered into two opposing coalitions: the Dual Alliance of Germany and Austria-Hungary, and the Triple Entente of Britain, France, and Russia. Tensions that had simmered for decades erupted in war in 1914. On June 28, terrorists from Serbia assassinated Austria-Hungary's heir to the throne, the Archduke Franz Ferdinand. Austria-Hungary declared war against Serbia on July 31. Russia entered the conflict against Serbia's side and mobilized its army against Austria-Hungary.

This triggered the alliance system: Germany declared war against Russia on August 1 and then against France two days later. Britain remained temporarily out of the conflict. That changed on August 4, when Germany sent troops into Belgium—a neutral country—in an effort to gain access to France's relatively weak northern border. The move drew Britain into the struggle because it had promised to defend Belgium under the 1839 Treaty of London. Britain declared war against Germany on August 4, 1914. What would soon become known as the Great War—and decades later as World War I—had begun.

Britain's declaration of war automatically drew all parts of its Empire into the conflict, including Newfoundland and Labrador. The dominion had not chosen to go to war, but the majority of its people, press, and government supported Britain's decision.

Approval was strongest in St. John's, where a large public celebration broke out on the night of August 6. "At the Post Office an immense crowd gathered and gave expression to a general outburst of patriotism," the *Evening Telegram* reported the next day. "About half-past ten a large number marched through the streets in processional order, singing patriotic songs and cheering at intervals. They visited Government House, where His Excellency delivered a short but stirring address brimful of patriotism."

Local newspapers received letters to the editor urging people to enlist in the Newfoundland Royal Naval Reserve or in other British forces. One of the earliest appeared in the *Daily News* on August 7, from a writer using the pseudonym "Cadet":

"It is not good enough for us to wait and rejoice in victories. We should prepare in our own small way to do our share and lose no time. The Naval Reserves are guarding the cable stations, but their numbers are not as large as we would wish them. All that is required is someone to lead, then we can get at least 1,000 able-bodied exercised men, who would be only too willing to volunteer and prepare for any emergency, and in case their services are needed abroad, then we will have a force to be counted upon. Now is the time for young Newfoundland to show the manhood of her sons."

The local media also overwhelmingly supported Britain and served as unofficial propagandists for its war effort. St. John's movie houses screened reels of King George V, British naval vessels, military leaders, and other patriotic images, while many newspapers printed emotional editorials that praised Britain, condemned Germany, and called upon the public to do its part.

"Much as we abhor and detest war with all its terrible consequences, Britons may

Western Star
SPECIAL
August 5, 1914

England Declares War Against Germany

England officially declared war on Germany 7.30 last night. German warships attacked scattered British fleet units in North Sea before war was declared, and wounded were landed at Scotland.

Wireless to Admiralty says that British fleet bottled up the German fleet north of Denmark.

King George to-day addressed a message to the Colonies expressing

appreciation of their spontaneous assurances that they will give fullest support to the Mother Country.

Half billion dollars voted for defense.

Germany shelling a Belgian city and her troops are advancing into French territory.

Japan remains faithful to British alliance.

well take pride in the firm conviction that the war was none of their seeking," the *Western Star* editorialized on August 12. "It was the culmination of the aggressive policy which has characterized German diplomacy for the past ten years."

The *Daily News* expanded on those sentiments the next day: "The war is not only one of defence against unjustifiable and unreasonable aggression, but it is a

THE DAILY NEWS.

EIGHT PAGES.   EIGHT PAGES.

VOL. 21 $3.00 Per Annum.   ST. JOHN'S, NEWFOUNDLAND, WEDNESDAY, AUGUST 5, 1914.   Price One Cent.   NO. 179

The British Empire is at War and all Europe is Ablaze.

War Declared at 7.30 O'Clock Last Night.

fight for the national existence, and for the liberties, the homes and the happiness of the people. Newfoundland is just as much threatened as any other part of the Empire. In one direction is glorious freedom under the British Flag; in the other, slavery and insult from an alien nation. Every young man who enrols his name on the list of Volunteers is offering his services for the protection of his family, his country, and his Empire."

Daily News, August 7 (left) and August 8 (right), 1914.

Rather than create a government war department and endure the tangle of red tape that would necessarily ensue, Davidson advocated for the formation of an extra-parliamentary volunteer organization to manage the proposed regiment. He reasoned that a volunteer association would take far less time and money to organize—and both were in short supply during the hasty days of early mobilization.

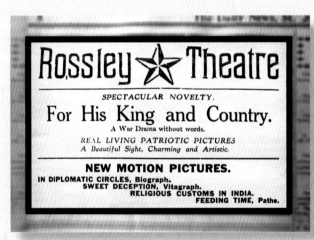

Patriotic films were the order of the day at local movie houses.
Daily News, August 31, 1914

It quickly became apparent that there was an abundance of men in Newfoundland and Labrador who wanted to serve overseas. On August 7, 50 members of the Legion of Frontiersmen jointly announced their intention to join the armed forces. Two days later, hundreds of current and former church brigade members also proclaimed their readiness.

It was initially assumed that volunteers would have to join British or Canadian armed forces, but the Newfoundland government was not content to simply provide recruits for other Allied forces. Four days after the war broke out, Newfoundland's governor, Sir Walter Davidson, sent a telegram to London requesting permission to establish a local regiment. The dominion, he wrote, could recruit 500 soldiers in a month and expand its Naval Reserve to 1,000 men by the end of October. London accepted both offers.

It was a considerable commitment from a small dominion and one that the government did not immediately know how to meet. Finding recruits would not be a problem (at least in the short term), but building the infrastructure needed to train, shelter, clothe, and feed them—and then ship them off to war and care for them when they returned—was a problem that the government would struggle to solve in the coming weeks, months, and years.

Governor Sir Walter Davidson
Before coming to Newfoundland in 1913, Governor Sir Walter Davidson had served at the crown colonies of Ceylon, Transvaal, and the Seychelles Islands. He had little experience with the system of responsible government in place in Newfoundland and was distasteful of partisan politics.

He believed that the governor should play a direct role in state administration and he wanted to take an active, rather than symbolic, role in administering the war effort. Davidson's willingness to contribute, combined with Prime Minister Morris's tenuous hold on power, made the two men question the benefits of forming a state-run military department.

7

NEWFOUNDLAND PATRIOTIC ASSOCIATION

NPA members with soldiers and sailors at the Regiment training camp in Pleasantville, St. John's, September 1914.
The Rooms Provincial Archives Division, F 30-26

include representatives from the People's Party and the official Opposition, then it would enjoy much broader support and hopefully less controversy than a government department.

A non-governmental organization would also make it unnecessary for Morris to co-operate with the Liberal and Union parties to manage the war effort. Morris was particularly loathe to put himself in a position of indebtedness to William Coaker, the leader of the Union Party, who would likely demand significant changes to fisheries policy in return for his support on key military decisions.

Further, Davidson himself strongly advocated for a volunteer organization. He was eager to play an active role in the dominion's war effort, but would remain a figurehead if a military department was in charge. However, if a volunteer association was formed, he could assume a key position and have considerable sway over the decision-making process.

With a government military department out of the picture, it was left to civilian volunteers to direct Newfoundland's war effort. Most had never seen a real soldier before 1914, but they rose to the challenge of building an army nonetheless. Thousands of men and women from across the dominion tackled virtually every aspect of the war effort. They performed core military tasks, like recruiting and training soldiers, and they did general work, like fundraising and sending care packages to servicemen overseas. It was in many ways a haphazard do-it-yourself mobilization.

Most of the volunteers were organized under two umbrella groups: the Newfoundland Patriotic Association (NPA) and the Women's Patriotic Association (WPA).

The first to form was the NPA, which essentially assumed the role of a government military department for the first three years

of the fighting. It was created by Governor Sir Walter Davidson, with support from Prime Minister Sir Edward Morris.

The two men favoured a non-partisan volunteer organization over a government department. They realized that a volunteer organization would be faster, easier, and cheaper to establish than a government-run military department. In August 1914, it was widely believed that the war would be over by Christmas, so why spend time and money forming a war department?

Morris and Davidson also believed that a volunteer association would be better able to unite people under a common cause. Newfoundland society was deeply divided along political and denominational lines. They recognized that if the new group's membership could bring together representatives from the dominion's three major denominations (Anglican, Roman Catholic, and Methodist), and

Coaker's Opposition

Notably absent from the NPA's membership was William Coaker. Davidson and Morris had invited Coaker to join the NPA, but he opposed the association. Coaker thought the government was ignoring its responsibilities by allowing a private organization to oversee military matters and argued that Morris should not allow a group of unelected citizens to decide how public money would be spent on the war effort. He also questioned why a seafaring dominion was devoting most of its resources to a land force instead of the Naval Reserve.

Coaker, however, was in the minority. The NPA received extensive support from Newfoundland's political, commercial, and social elite and from the St. John's public in general. The government willingly allowed the group to take charge of the war effort.

Finally, public response to a volunteer organization was favourable, particularly in St. John's. When Davidson chaired a public meeting on August 12 to discuss forming the association, more than 3,000 people (representing a cross-section of the population) attended, and passed the resolution.

The NPA officially formed five days later. Davidson became its leader and its members included some of the more influential people in the dominion. Representatives from the three major Christian denominations joined and so did officials from the People's Party and the Opposition Liberals. Merchants, lawyers, judges,

EUROPEAN WAR TO BE THE SHORTEST ON RECORD

Is the Opinion of Experts

doctors, newspaper editors, and city councillors signed on. So did the handful of people on the island able to lend military advice: officials from the Newfoundland Royal Naval Reserve, the St. John's Rifle Club, and local paramilitary groups.

The association was concentrated in St. John's, but outport magistrates, journalists, politicians, and doctors also formed branches in 45 rural communities.

Members of the Newfoundland Regiment at Fort William, ca. 1915–1918.
The Rooms Provincial Archives Division, NA 2744

The group's first and founding role was to establish a Newfoundland regiment. It created various committees to take on specific tasks such as officer selection, finance, and recruiting and training. As needs arose, more committees were formed.

The NPA's responsibilities quickly expanded to include virtually every aspect of Newfoundland's war effort. It became responsible for soldier pensions and disability payments, veterans' hospitals, and civil re-establishment programs. It helped to recruit volunteers to the Newfoundland Royal Naval Reserve and to the Newfoundland Forestry Corps after that unit was formed in 1917.

It also became involved in an array of fundraising drives, which helped pay for a wide range of needs that included warplanes for British forces, medical supplies for Allied hospitals, and Christmas gifts for troops overseas.

For the first year and a half of its existence, the NPA united political parties and religious groups under a common cause. But the war dragged on longer than anyone anticipated and administrating the dominion's role in it was unexpectedly complex.

By the summer of 1916, the NPA was struggling to maintain the Newfoundland Regiment at full battalion strength. One year later, conscription seemed inevitable. The Newfoundland government recognized that it could not allow a private organization to draft troops, so it created a department of militia in the summer of 1917 to take over responsibility from the NPA. Although the association gradually disappeared in the coming months, many of its volunteers found new roles in the department of militia.

Tent City

Although far removed from the European front lines, the city of St. John's often assumed the character of a war camp during the war. Thousands of soldiers, sailors, and foresters assembled at St. John's throughout the war to be dispatched overseas. St. John's residents gathered at the Regiment's camp near Quidi Vidi Lake to watch the men train; countless banquets, socials, and farewell parties were held and open to the public. The majority of the Newfoundland Regiment's early recruits came from the city, many from the ranks of its cadet corps.

WOMEN'S PATRIOTIC ASSOCIATION

The second volunteer group powering Newfoundland's war effort was the Women's Patriotic Association (WPA), an island-wide organization with more than 15,000 members. It raised money, shipped clothing and other goods to troops, volunteered in local hospitals, and visited families who had loved ones overseas. The WPA also collaborated with international groups such as the Red Cross and St. John Ambulance Association.

Lady Margaret Davidson, wife of Governor Sir Walter Davidson, founded the WPA at a public meeting in St. John's on August 31, 1914. She outlined the group's purpose to the more than 700 women who attended:

"We have received an appeal from the St. John Ambulance Association asking

WPA volunteers at Government House. *The Rooms Provincial Archives Division, B 5-173*

for things for the sick and wounded and they sent a list of the things required, which comprise shirts, cotton and flannel, not flannelette, bed jackets, pyjama sleeping suits, pillows, pillow slips and old linen, not old clothes. Now I feel sure we women in Newfoundland can help in this way with our work, as well as in other ways and we shall do so best and most effectively if we join together and cooperate. To do this, I consider that we shall do best to organize ourselves into an Association."

WPA branches quickly sprang up across the island and the membership bridged the class and religious gaps that had divided Newfoundland society for generations. Volunteers included the very

wealthy and the very poor. They came from outport communities and from commercial centres, and they belonged to almost every religious denomination that existed in the dominion.

One exception was the group's executive members, who came from the dominion's richest and most distinguished families. Branch presidents were usually the wives of doctors, merchants, ministers, and other prominent figures.

One year after the association was formed, WPA secretary Eleanor MacPherson outlined its rapid progress:

"There are now fully organized and working along lines very much the same as we have adopted in St. John's, 168 branches. In very few cases have there been any divisions, but dropping all distinctions of a social or religious nature, the women have joined hands to work for the men at the front. It has been estimated (not by the society) but by some one rather good at figures that there are something over 15,000 women in Newfoundland who are doing their bit! Inspiring, is it not?"

One of the WPA's central goals was to provide Newfoundland and Labrador servicemen with material comforts from home. Chocolate and tobacco were important treats, but clothing made up the bulk of many WPA care packages. All across the island, thousands of women knitted socks, mittens, sweaters, and scarves and sewed flannel shirts, pyjamas, and other clothes.

The Newfoundland Sock
The WPA's grey wool socks became an icon of wartime Newfoundland. Soldiers, such as Private Frank Lind of the Newfoundland Regiment, praised them in the letters they sent home. "The Newfoundland sock is the best in the world and it is prized by every soldier," Lind wrote from France on April 22, 1916. "How many times at the peninsula and before we ever saw Egypt have regiment soldiers asked if we had a pair of Newfoundland socks to give or sell them?" Some said the WPA would "win the war in knitting socks, still socks, and always more SOCKS!"

The Daily News. St. John's

WOMEN'S PATRIOTIC ASSOCIATION

SEVEN HUNDRED RESPOND TO CALL

STIRRING ADDRESS BY LADY DAVIDSON

His Excellency Explains the Situation

If the attendance, at yesterday's meeting convened by Lady Davidson be any criterion of the willingness of Newfoundland women to assist in aiding Britain in the present crisis by providing for our soldiers at the front, then such assistance is assured, for long before the appointed hour the hall was thronged. Lady Davidson in opening the meeting delivered the following address:

LADY DAVIDSON'S ADDRESS

Friends:
Let me first say how very glad I

money orders they contained, and it was most touching to read some of these slips of paper containing several names subscribed to a 2s. (50 cts.) with the addition "We wish we could give more, and we are so sorry for those fine fellows in Nfld." —the post mark on one occasion I remember to be Ramsgate, a fishing town on the E. coast, and we felt sure it came from a poor fisherman's family— probably now all the stalwart lads of that family, as of many others have been called to arms.

As I have already said—this is a unique time when we are called up-

Distaff, 1916 (photo); *Daily News*, September 1, 1914.

By the time peace was restored on November 11, 1918, the WPA had collected more than $500,000—about $6.5 million in 2016. It was a staggering amount from such a small dominion. Only about 250,000 people lived in Newfoundland and Labrador, many of whom were poor.

Politicians, the press, and the public praised the WPA's work and, in 1918, King George V awarded the prestigious Order of the British Empire to nine WPA members for their contributions to the war effort.

The WPA's high profile and reputation would later help effect significant social change. During the war, it had demonstrated that women's traditional roles—such as caregiving and knitting—were of tremendous economic and social importance. When the fighting ended, many WPA members adopted a new mission: to win voting rights for women.

The WPA dissolved in 1921, but reformed 18 years later to coordinate volunteer work for World War II.

They were prolific workers, who by 1916 had produced 62,000 pairs of socks, 9,000 shirts, 6,000 pairs of gloves, and 2,400 scarves.

WPA volunteers performed many other jobs too. They kept in touch with families who had soldiers or sailors fighting overseas and they visited troops recovering in local hospitals. By the end of 1916, WPA volunteers had paid more than 4,500 visits to homes and hospitals.

The WPA was also a powerful fundraiser. It published the *Distaff* magazine to raise money for the Red Cross and to publicize the work that women were doing during the war. WPA volunteers sold calendars, Christmas stamps, and flowers, and they organized music concerts, hockey games, and other events— anything that might bring in money for the war.

Appreciate Comforts From Home.

Mrs. Jas. Gushue, Patrick Street, has received a pleasing sovenir of France from No. 821 Sergt. J. A. Taylor, one of our soldiers on active service. He recently found a note written by her in her pocket of a shirt she had made for the W.P.A. He thanked her for her kind wishes, and assured her that comforts from home are always very much appreciated by the boys of the regiment.

Evening Telegram, July 14, 1917.

Warm Words inside Warm Socks

Hidden inside many sock heels or shirt pockets was a handwritten note from the WPA knitter to the soldier who would receive her handiwork. The messages usually contained words of encouragement or a brief prayer and the knitter's home address. Many soldiers wrote back to say thank you.

Thanks for Socks

Somewhere in France
May 23rd. 1918
Dear Miss Clarke:— Just a note thanking you for the socks which were very nice indeed and in such a place as France. I know the people in Twillingate must work hard working for the soldiers of Nfld. I don't know if I know any of your friends out here but I can tell you that all the boys that are here at present are feeling well. My address is 83 E. G. NOFTALL, 1st Royal Nfld. Regt. B.E.F. France.

Your friend, Ted.

Twillingate Sun, July 6, 1918.

PART TWO
THE ROYAL NEWFOUNDLAND REGIMENT

"When we go to the front, it will not be one Newfoundlander today and one tomorrow etc., but suddenly you may hear of a whole Company being wiped out."

—*Lieutenant Owen Steele, May 30, 1915*

"I wish I could illustrate to you just what it is like ... how calmly one stands and faces death, jokes and laughs; everything is just an everyday occurrence. You are mud covered, dry and caked, perhaps, but you look at the chap next you and laugh at the state he is in; then you look down at your own clothes and then the other fellow laughs. Then a whizz bang comes across and misses both of you, and both laugh together."

—*Private Frank Lind, June 29, 1916*

tember 26, 970 men had enlisted. Of those, 565 were accepted, more than 200 rejected, and the remainder held for further consideration. Those who passed the medical and other requirements moved into a training camp the NPA had established in St. John's. These recruits became known as the First Five Hundred. The majority of them were former or current members of the church brigades and the Legion of Frontiersmen.

The NPA met its quota of 500 soldiers with ease, but it struggled to outfit, train, and shelter them. After recruiting opened, the first order of business was to find a place where the men would live and train. The NPA decided to convert a cricket field near Quidi Vidi Lake into a military camp. Local businesses, church

Volunteers of the Newfoundland Regiment at target practice at Quidi Vidi, 1914.
The Rooms Provincial Archives Division, VA 37-5.4

The Newfoundland Regiment has been called the dominion's first great national effort. In 1914, a dominion that had no military forces of its own created an infantry unit that would go on to fight in some of the most savage battles of World War I. By the time hostilities ended, the men of the Newfoundland Regiment had gained a reputation for courage and determination in the face of enormous danger. Their valour and their heartbreaking sacrifice won the Regiment the prestigious title of *Royal* and the devotion of the Newfoundland and Labrador people.

But the unit had humble beginnings. On August 21, 1914, the Newfoundland Regiment issued a call for recruits. It wanted 500 men between the ages of 19 and 35, weighing at least 120 pounds and at least 5 feet 4 inches tall. They had to be healthy enough to pass a medical exam (many could not).

Recruits were paid one dollar a day, which was on par with what Canadian soldiers earned and far above the one shilling per day (about 20 cents) paid to British soldiers. In return, enlistees committed to "serv[ing] abroad for the duration of the war, but not exceeding one year." A full 12 months of service seemed unlikely at the time, as military experts predicted that fighting would be over by Christmas.

Some men signed up for the money—the economy was faltering and unemployment high—some out of a patriotic desire to defend the British Empire, and some for the imagined adventure of fighting in far-off lands. Many joined for all three reasons.

Whatever the motivation, the early response exceeded all expectations. About 335 volunteers came forward in the first week and, by the time recruiting for the first contingent ended on Sep-

A Ragtag Bunch of Blue Puttees

Clothing the First Five Hundred proceeded in a haphazard manner. A shortage of military headgear forced most early recruits to use civilian hats or go bareheaded until they landed overseas. The NPA had ordered Australian-style slouch hats from Montreal, but these had not arrived before the first contingent left the island. Fortunately, the greatcoats imported from Montreal arrived in time to keep troops warm during their fall training.

The Newfoundland government and NPA decided that, wherever possible, local companies would be hired to manufacture clothing and equipment, which included boots, blankets, underwear, grey flannel shirts, and uniforms. This was good for local businesses, but it created unforeseen difficulties.

As there was not enough khaki serge on the island to make dress uniforms, early recruits were issued fatigues made from a light cotton material known as khaki drill. They also wound navy blue puttees around their lower legs because the NPA's clothing committee decided to go with that colour instead of the regulation khaki. The non-standard leg coverings became a badge of distinction for the First Five Hundred and earned the men a second nickname—the Blue Puttees.

brigades, and private citizens donated hundreds of tents; still more had to be made from sails taken from vessels in the harbour. The pulp and paper company in Grand Falls, the Anglo-Newfoundland Development (AND) Company, provided wooden tent floors, while the Anglo-American Telegraph Company installed telephones. The first recruits arrived on September 1 and all 565 were in tents by the end of the month.

Finding enough weapons and gear presented a greater challenge. Rifles were in short supply on the island as were machine guns, revolvers, binoculars, and almost every other piece of equipment needed to send an infantry unit to war. The NPA ordered 500 rifles from Canada and 100 revolvers from Britain. Newfoundland's isolation and the limitations of early 20th-century shipping presented obstacles. The revolvers were delivered on August 29, but the rifles did not arrive until after the first contingent had left Newfoundland for England on October 4.

Other items necessary for battle were gathered from what was locally available, and with invaluable help from the public. The Newfoundland Royal Naval Reserve loaned the Regiment service rifles and ammunition, and the church brigades provided miniature rifles for target practice. In January 1915, the Reid Newfoundland Company donated two Vickers machine guns to the Regiment—they were so large that a team of about six men was required to operate them. The donation was a windfall for the Regiment because the guns were vital to training, but prohibitively expensive at about $2,000 each.

The public showed its support again later that year, when donations to the NPA's Machine Gun Fund enabled the Regiment to buy six more Vickers guns.

Throughout September, the men studied the basics of military service. They went on foot marches, learned how to use bayonets and other weapons, practiced marksmanship and skirmishing, followed

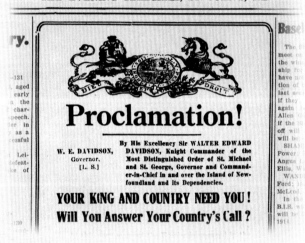

THE EVENING TELEGRAM, ST. JOHN'S, NL

Proclamation!

W. E. DAVIDSON, Governor, [L. S.]

By His Excellency Sir WALTER EDWARD DAVIDSON, Knight Commander of the Most Distinguished Order of St. Michael and St. George, Governor and Commander-in-Chief in and over the Island of Newfoundland and its Dependencies.

YOUR KING AND COUNTRY NEED YOU!
Will You Answer Your Country's Call ?

a physical fitness routine, and acquired the basic skills of being a soldier. Their training was generally confined to three locations: the military camp at Quidi Vidi Lake, a rifle range on the south side of the harbour, and the White Hills—an area just east of Quidi Vidi where they practiced skirmishing. They also marched through the city streets, much

to the delight of local residents who watched and cheered the processions.

Public support for the Regiment was strong throughout the city. Crowds frequently gathered at the military camp to watch recruits train and to photograph the men. The NPA encouraged this behaviour as a way to maintain public support for the war effort. It even printed ads in newspapers asking people to send in their photographs so it could compile a regimental photo album.

But there were times when military and civilian activities clashed. The rifle range was near a popular berry patch and training began at the peak of the picking season. Notices appeared in local newspapers warning berry-pickers to avoid the firing zone.

On October 3, 1914, the First Five Hundred marched to the St. John's waterfront and boarded the *Florizel*. As not all of the 565 original recruits had completed their training, only about 540 boarded the steamer (different reports peg the number anywhere from 525 to 546 men).

Thousands of people lined the streets to say farewell. Bunting hung from windows and marching band music filled the air. The men, who were divided into A and B Companies, had completed the St. John's portion of their training and were on their way to the United Kingdom, where superior facilities and more experienced military personnel could better prepare them for war. The *Florizel* set sail on October 4. Many of the recruits had never left the island before. Now they were headed to a distant land to fight a distant war.

The *Florizel*

The *Florizel* was an unusual choice for a troopship. The icebreaker had been built in 1909 to carry passengers and cargo between St. John's, Halifax, and New York and to participate in the annual spring seal hunt at the North Atlantic ice floes. It was intended for relatively short-distance travel in icy waters, not to transport 500 men across the Atlantic Ocean. But as the *Florizel* was available on short notice, the NPA and the Newfoundland Regiment made do. It was an unconventional troopship for unconventional troops, who boarded it bareheaded, in blue puttees, and without rifles (which arrived in St. John's 12 hours after the *Florizel* had departed).

"Making do" was something the Blue Puttees raised to an art form aboard the *Florizel*. The vessel had been quickly converted and comfort was sacrificed to function. "Really the conditions under which we found ourselves on coming aboard, owing to utter lack of preparation, were simply scandalous," Lieutenant Arthur Wakefield later reported to the governor's office. "Arrangements for the men's accommodation for sleeping, messing, washing and latrines were ridiculously insufficient, or entirely lacking.… It was impossible to find sleeping accommodation for the men till we discovered a large empty hold, where there are now nearly 100 living, sleeping and eating, in semi-darkness, and without any convenience of any kind except the tables which were hastily brought by our men from Pleasantville. An hour's work originally would at any rate have given the men electric light and cleanliness. *No extra washing or latrine accommodation of any kind had been provided!*"

Most subsequent drafts did not cross the Atlantic aboard the *Florizel* but instead travelled to Britain on more conventional troopships.

On October 20, the recruits said a not-so-fond farewell to the *Florizel*. They disembarked at Devonport in southern England and travelled by rail to a large military training camp at Salisbury Plain. It was unlike anything the men had ever experienced. Salisbury Plain was one of the largest military training grounds in the United Kingdom and accommodated thousands of soldiers from across the British Empire. It was a far cry from the cricket field in St. John's where the Blue Puttees had trained. The men were now only too aware of the immense scale of the war they were about to enter.

realizes also what a very serious undertaking is being carried on."

The Blue Puttees had arrived at Salisbury Plain during one of the coldest and wettest autumns the region had ever experienced—the rain was so unrelenting that the mud was sometimes knee-deep. Despite the discomforts, the men trained hard and their days were filled with physical exercise, rifle practice, skirmishes, and marching.

The Regiment stayed at Salisbury Plain for seven weeks before moving to Fort George in northern Scotland for further training. It was a welcome change from the mud and rain that had up until then

The Newfoundland Regiment at Stobs Camp in Scotland, 1915.
The Rooms Provincial Archives Division, VA 37-17.2

"All around our present camping ground are fully 3,000 tents, whilst as many more are visible within a mile or two of us," Sergeant (later Lieutenant) Owen Steele wrote in his diary on December 2, 1914. "When one realizes that these tents are the present habitations of thousands and thousands of men, all busily and earnestly undergoing strenuous training with the object of fighting for the honour, and maybe, the preservation of our great nation, one then

saturated their time in England. No longer in tents, the men bunked inside the fort's buildings. They also enjoyed a less rigorous training schedule because the shortened winter hours had come into effect. Recruits woke at 7 a.m.—an hour later than in the summer—and trained for three hours in the morning, followed by two more hours after lunch. On some days, they completed 34-kilometre route-marches in full military gear.

"There we felt more at home," Captain John Edward Joseph Fox wrote in *The Veteran* magazine. "In the first place we were decently housed, in the barracks of the Seaforth Highlanders; secondly, the climate was excellent and not unlike that of Newfoundland at its best; finally, we were within reasonable distance of civilization, for the towns of Nairn and Inverness were but a few miles away, and Scottish hospitality, as we were to discover, was in a class by itself."

But they were saddened on January 1, 1915, when Private John Fielding Chaplin died from an abdominal disease. The 19-year-old was the first soldier the Newfoundland Regiment lost.

On February 19, the Regiment was transferred to Edinburgh. Much of its time there was spent in training, but the men also guarded Edinburgh Castle, an honour never before given to an overseas unit.

Newfoundland soldiers at Stobs Camp, 1915.
The Rooms Provincial Archives Division, VA 37-35.3

The men remained at Stobs Camp until August 1915, when they were finally ready for active service. Soon, the brutal realities of trench warfare would make even the mud of Salisbury Plain seem like a holiday resort.

Subsequent recruits followed a training routine that was similar to the First Five Hundred's. They did preliminary training in St. John's and then spent several weeks of additional training in the UK before entering active service.

Identity Crisis

Much to the chagrin of the men of the Newfoundland Regiment, other Allied forces frequently confused them with Canadian soldiers. On October 12, 1914, the British battle cruiser *Princess Royal* passed by the *Florizel* and tried to honour its men by playing "O Canada." The Blue Puttees were not impressed.

The problem intensified at Salisbury Plain, where the Newfoundland Regiment was initially attached to the 4th Canadian Infantry Brigade. The move sparked rumours that the two units would eventually become one. "There was a general fear that our identity would be lost in a merger with some Canadian unit," Captain John Edward Joseph Fox later wrote for *The Veteran*. "Not that we had developed a 'superiority complex' so far as our neighbours were concerned, but we felt, quite properly, that if we were to give our best we could only do so by preserving our own individuality."

Concerns were put to rest in early December, when Allied commanders ordered the Newfoundland Regiment to Fort George in northern Scotland for further training and sent the Canadian Infantry Brigade to France.

"All the boys are well and happy, and who wouldn't be happy under the circumstances," Private Frank Lind wrote to the editor of the St. John's *Daily News* in a letter dated February 20, 1915: "Why here we are, the 750 of us, the guard over this wonderful Castle (for the Scotch regiment left on our arrival). We are—in a way—monarchs of all we survey. Isn't it a great honour for us Newfoundland boys to be in charge of this grand old place? What we shall have to tell you all when we get back, and please God, we hope to all return again."

On May 11, 1915, the Regiment left Edinburgh and proceeded to Stobs Camp in southern Scotland. The men were once again under canvas and following a rigorous training schedule, which Lind described in another letter to the *Daily News* on May 20, 1915: "by the time we leave here this will be a body of men 'hard as nails', for we are hard at drill from 5:30 a.m. until 4:30 p.m., skirmishing, squad-drill, company drill and physical exercise."

Newfoundland Regiment soldiers. *The Rooms Provincial Archives Division, F-48-4*

18

Soon after the Blue Puttees departed Newfoundland, the government and the NPA decided to expand the Regiment to full battalion strength, which would require about 1,080 men in the field and another 500 in reserve. It was a significant commitment from a small dominion, and one that was made quickly, with little consideration of how the NPA could sustain a steady supply of recruits if the fighting lasted longer than the anticipated few months.

Newfoundland and Labrador had a population of about 250,000 in 1914. Of the approximately 122,500 males, only 33,708 were old enough for military service. Medical, physical, and other requirements further narrowed the pool of eligible volunteers. Economic barriers were also an issue. The cod fishery was the mainstay of the Newfoundland economy and needed an ample supply of able-bodied men. Many fishers could not go overseas without plunging their families into poverty; nor could the dominion afford to lose too many fishers to the front lines.

Nonetheless, the NPA issued a call for recruits to the second contingent of the Newfoundland Regiment on November 26, 1914. With the exception of increasing the maximum age limit to 36, the eligibility requirements remained the same. The war was still in its early stages and the public's enthusiasm for volunteering remained high. In just three days, 433 men had signed up; by December 10, there were 607.

By then, the NPA was better equipped to outfit and train volunteers. Khaki material had arrived in sufficiently large quantities and there were many more rifles, machine guns, and other equipment at the Regiment's disposal.

All new recruits trained at St. John's for several weeks before travelling to the UK. A group of approximately 250 men (C Company) departed Newfoundland aboard the SS *Dominion* on February 5, 1915. By April 1916, five more companies (D through H) of about 250 men each had gone overseas.

Most outport men who joined the Newfoundland Regiment were part of these later companies. The rapid pace of early mobilization had excluded many rural residents from the First Five Hundred because they had to travel significant distances to train in St. John's. A scarcity of newspapers outside the dominion's larger centres also made it difficult for news to reach potential recruits in rural areas. Also, outport residents were seafarers, and many preferred to join the Newfoundland Royal Naval Reserve (about 2,000 did during the war).

The NPA itself contributed to low enlistment rates in rural areas by failing to communicate with residents in a meaningful way. Few of its 45 outport branches had existed for more than a year. The NPA remained an essentially St. John's-oriented organization and failed to recognize the significant economic and geographic barriers that prevented rural residents from enlisting.

Outport families depended on the seasonal cod fishery for their livelihoods, and if the men left their homes to enlist, their families would suffer financial hardship. The NPA provided little aid to offset this problem. It was a different story in the city, where some businesses promised to reserve jobs for employees who enlisted and to top up their military pay so it would equal their usual salaries back home.

The government's weak presence in rural areas also undermined the NPA's ability to enlist volunteers. This became clear to a recruiter who visited Sop's Island in White Bay in the fall of 1916. Unable to enlist a single person, he reported to the *Evening Telegram* on January 8, 1917: "For all the public service the residents get, they might well be forgiven if they failed to appreciate that they belonged to any Empire or to any group of persons outside of themselves."

Even more obstacles prevented Labradorians from signing up. Many had to travel across hundreds of kilometres of difficult terrain before they could even reach the coast. They also had to time their journey so they could arrive between the sailing of the first coastal boat in the spring and the last one in the fall. Motivation was another barrier. Government services were almost non-existent in Labrador and its people could not even vote in the dominion's elections. Why fight in a war that distant governments waged in a distant land?

Some Labradorians lived in areas so remote that they did not even know the war had begun until months after the fact. News was slow to arrive, but recruiters were slower still—no formal recruiting effort was launched in Labrador until March 1915 when Dr. Wilfred Grenfell agreed to enlist volunteers for the Newfoundland Regiment.

Grenfell, who had served in Labrador since 1892, had established a string of hospitals and nursing stations along its coast. He was well positioned to identify suitable recruits because he knew many of the local people and could visit prospective soldiers on his frequent journeys up and down the Labrador coast in his medical ship.

The traditional skills of many Labradorians made them valuable soldiers. Many were trappers and hunters. They were good marksmen who were used to spending long stretches of time outside, living in rough conditions with little shelter from the elements. All of this came in handy in the trenches of World War I.

John Shiwak

One of Labrador's most famous recruits was an Inuk hunter and trapper from Rigolet. John Shiwak was 26 years old when he enlisted on July 24, 1915. He became known as one of the Newfoundland Regiment's best snipers—a skill he attributed to his experience shooting seals as they surfaced to breathe.

Shiwak quickly earned a promotion to the rank of Lance Corporal, but the violence of war took a heavy toll. In letters to his friends and family, Shiwak questioned the slaughter of the trenches and described an aching loneliness.

"My Dear Louisa," he wrote his girlfriend from the front lines in France, "I have only time to write you a postcard today. I am in the best of health. Hope you are the same and not too lonely. I wonder if you think of me any time during all this lonely time since I left you last summer. Write and let me know if you are still true. I think of you every day even when I am in the line. I would love to see you now dear."

Lance Corporal John Shiwak was killed in the Battle of Cambrai on November 20, 1917.

One full year of fighting passed before Allied commanders deployed the Newfoundland Regiment to an active front. In August 1915, the unit received word that it was going to Suvla Bay in the Gallipoli Peninsula. There, the Regiment would join the 88th Brigade of the 29th Division of the British Army.

This peninsula was strategically important because of its proximity to a narrow strait of water called the Dardanelles, which provided a sea route to Russia. The Allied powers wanted to seize control of the area from Turkey, and dispatched thousands of troops to the region in 1915.

The Newfoundland Regiment left Devonport, England, on August 20 and arrived at Alexandria, Egypt, on September 1. It then travelled by train to Cairo. The men spent two weeks in Egypt, acclimating to the stifling heat they would encounter at Gallipoli.

On September 14, they set sail for Suvla Bay. Most of them were happy to be finally out of training, but there was also an awareness of the pending danger. "We have had a very good time all along so far, but we all know that the hardest part has now to come," Lieutenant Owen Steele wrote in his diary on September 18, 1915. "The place where we are to land is shelled all day long, and the last Division which went there lost 1,200 men and 36 officers the *first day*, and that, without having fired a shot, nor seen a single Turk, so we have heard."

The Regiment's 1,076 men landed on the shores of the Dardanelles at about 3 a.m. on September 20, 1915. They came under immediate fire from Turkish troops. Private Francis Lind described his first day at Gallipoli in a letter to the *Daily News* on September 27, 1915: "We have had quite a lively time since landing Monday morning amidst a storm of shot and shell. After reaching the shore we made a rush and getting out our trenching tools began to dig ourselves in. The shells were falling thick about us.... One

shell burst about five feet from our dug-out; we only just 'ducked' in time. Another knocked Sergt. Green's helmet off, and it went about twenty feet away. He has never seen it since."

The Newfoundland Regiment lost its first men in battle soon after arriving at Suvla Bay: Private Hugh McWhirter was 21 years old when a Turkish shell killed him on September 22, 1915; the next day, a sniper's bullet killed 22-year-old Private William Hardy.

By September 30, the Newfoundland Regiment had taken responsibility for a 1.5-kilometre stretch of the British front line. Its trenches lay just 50 metres from the Turkish lines, and they jutted out at an angle that exposed the men to enemy fire from two sides.

Men of the Newfoundland Regiment in front-line trenches at Suvla Bay, 1915. *The Rooms Provincial Archives Division, VA 37-1.1 and VA 37-1.3*

"After the first forty-eight hours we settled down to regular trench warfare," Lance Corporal John Gallishaw wrote in *Trenching at Gallipoli*: "The routine was four days in the trenches, eight days in rest dugouts, four days in the trenches again, and so forth, although three or four months later our ranks were so depleted that we stayed in eight days and rested only four."

Turkish forces frequently shelled the Regiment, but there were other threats. The trenches were filthy and overcrowded, and No Man's Land was littered with bodies. Disease and illness spread among the men. Gallishaw reported that about 600 Turkish bodies lay on the ground near B Company's trenches, but no one could retrieve and bury them without exposing himself to enemy fire: "We could not get out to bury them, nor could we afford to allow the enemy to do so.

Pte. Hugh Walter McWhirter, killed at Gallipoli on September 22, 1915. *ASC, Coll. 346 1.01.025*

The Letters of Private Frank Lind

Excerpts from letters sent to the *Daily News*.

Somewhere in the Dardanelles,

September 27th, 1915

I am writing this in my "dug-out," perhaps you know what that is, and possibly some of your readers don't. A "dug-out" is a place dug in the ground large enough for a man to lie down, and sometimes after going down three or four feet or more we dig in, and make a cave, and there we may lie back comfortably and fill our pipe with "Mayo" [tobacco] if we have any, and smile at the shells bursting on the roof overhead.

At present the shells are coming fast and thick, some whistling by, others bursting somewhere where we might be but for this very convenient "dug-out." If it were not for the dug-outs we would have to stay in the open ground exposed until a shell dropped near us, and then we would likely go somewhere else—in sections—which would be rather unpleasant.

Somewhere in the Dardanelles,

October 13th, 1915

Up to present as near as I can judge, we have, besides sick, about sixty wounded and eight dead. Two of our fellows died of dysentery,—Lance-Corporal Watts of A Co., and Pte. Walter Murphy of No. 8 Platoon, B Company. Walter was in our platoon and we all miss him so much, such a quiet unassuming fellow, he was liked by everybody. His brother, Mike, is in C Company.

We won't be sorry to get to the dug-outs tomorrow for a brief rest. We look forward with pleasure to the fact that tomorrow night we may take off our boots when retiring. Oh, delicious thought, it makes us happy all over, and if any of your readers want to get a small idea of what a comfort it is, just let him sleep in his clothes, in his comfortable bed, not in a trench, for say two days, not two or three weeks, and ask him how it feels,—yes, even to remove his boots only. Some day no doubt we will be able to remove our tunic and pants, and yes, perhaps, our shirt, and even have a wash. When that time comes I shall certainly have to ask somebody to pinch me to make sure that I am not dreaming.

Somewhere in Gallipoli,

October 14, 1915

We have had some narrow escapes amongst our fellows. Private Hoddinott, when picking up a wounded man, felt a sting in the crown of his head, and discovered that a bullet had gone through his helmet and just grazed his skull. Will Taylor had a bullet rip through the collar of his tunic and not do him a bit of harm. Half an inch the other way, or less, would have done for each of them. R.C. Grieve had a bullet in his cheek, a nasty wound, but he will be O.K. in a few days.

There they stayed, and some of the hordes of flies that continually hovered about them, with every change of wind, swept down into our trenches, carrying to our food the germs of dysentery, enteric, and all the foul diseases that threaten men in the tropics."

The weather was another problem, especially after the rainy season began in October. Sudden squalls drenched the men's clothes and flooded the trenches. The days remained hot, but the nights grew bitterly cold. Rheumatism and pneumonia became serious threats. The situation deteriorated on November 26, when a flood struck Suvla Bay and was followed by a deep freeze.

"On the night of the flood, the water in our support trenches and in the firing line was three feet deep nearly everywhere," Steele wrote on December 4. "Then when the frost came, it tried us all to the limit and all suffered severely ... We have sent about 150 men to hospital, most of them being for frost burnt feet. We have heard that the 86th Brigade lost 200 men by drowning and exposure and nearly 2,000 were sent to hospital."

Despite the dangers and squalor of trench warfare, the Regiment won its first battle honours at Gallipoli. On the night of November 4, Lieutenant James Donnelly led seven men to a ridge held by Turkish snipers. They fought off three snipers and held the area until reinforcements arrived the following morning.

The ridge was renamed Caribou Hill in the Regiment's honour. Donnelly was later awarded the Military Cross, while Lance Corporal Fred Snow received the Distinguished Conduct Medal.

In the end, the Allied forces could not wrestle control of Suvla Bay from the Turkish Army, and evacuated the area between December 18, 1915, and January 9, 1916.

Lieut. James John Donnelly.
The Rooms Provincial Archives Division, VA 36-1.4

The Gallipoli Campaign had reduced the Newfoundland Regiment to 17 officers and 470 other ranks. Forty-four of its men had died and hundreds more were recovering from enemy fire or disease in military hospitals. The Regiment withdrew to Egypt for two months of training and recuperation.

In the spring, the Newfoundland Regiment was ordered to the River Somme in northern France. It would soon take part in one of the largest and deadliest battles of World War I.

CLUNY MACPHERSON'S GAS MASK

World War I triggered an arms race between the Allied forces and the Central powers. As each side tried to gain the upper hand, their best scientists and military experts searched for new weapons and new tactics. Tanks and flame-throwers appeared on the battlefields, guns were invented for airplanes, and the first underwater bombs sought out submarines.

Cluny Macpherson (centre) in Egypt, ca. 1915
The Rooms Provincial Archives Division, A 24-155

There was also poison gas. Scientists had long understood its military potential, but it had never been used on a large scale before this war. On April 22, 1915, the Germans attacked French troops with 168 tons of chlorine gas on a battlefield at Ypres. The 6-kilometre-wide yellow-green cloud could smother men in 10 minutes. About 5,000 French soldiers died that day and another 2,000 became prisoners of war (POWs). Many of the survivors were temporarily blinded.

Allied forces scrambled to find a defence against this devastating weapon. It arrived a few weeks later in the form of a gas mask—a cloth hood that covered the eyes, nose, and mouth and filtered out any dangerous chemicals. Its inventor: Doctor Cluny Macpherson from Newfoundland.

Macpherson began his wartime service as the Newfoundland Regiment's Principal Medical Officer. Soon after the Germans launched their surprise gas attack in April 1915, Allied leaders invited him to join an international team of scientists who were searching for a defence against future gas attacks.

One of the team's first solutions was based on a rudimentary gas mask that the Germans had been wearing during the attack. It was basically a cotton pad soaked in a chemical solution that rendered chlorine gas harmless. Macpherson later wrote in his notebook that he thought the design would be ineffective in battle: "I thought hard on the whole subject and came to the conclusion that, while the German pattern respirator could perhaps save one's life if one could stay still with one's hands busy keeping the pad just right to breathe through and with one's eyes shut to protect them, something else was needed to prevent the Germans following up their gas and wiping us out."

His suspicions were confirmed when he and his fellow researchers tested the masks: "Next morning with our Chlorine and German-pattern masks, Professors Watson and Baker with an officer and a few men went to some trenches outside town and, donning the masks, we released some of the Chlorine. The result was disastrous. Professor Watson was so badly gassed he was taken to a Canadian Hospital nearby. Professor Baker and I got more than was comfortable into our lungs and our eyes were pretty sore."

Cluny Macpherson before the War
Cluny Macpherson, born in St. John's on March 18, 1879, received his early education at the city's Methodist College and studied medicine at McGill University in Montreal.

Soon after graduation, Macpherson travelled to Labrador to work for the Royal National Mission to Deep Sea Fishermen, a charitable organization that provided medical services to people in remote locations. Macpherson became head of its hospital at Battle Harbour; there he helped to contain a smallpox epidemic that threatened the region.

After a few years in Labrador, Macpherson returned to his hometown of St. John's and opened a private medical practice. He also established a local branch of the St. John Ambulance Brigade—an international, semi-military, volunteer organization that provided first aid and other medical services in emergency situations.

In May 1915, Macpherson designed a mask that covered the entire face—it was essentially a cloth bag soaked in a chlorine-blocking hypo solution. The wearer could pull the bag over his head and tuck the bottom inside his shirt collar. It also had an eyepiece made from transparent film.

The other researchers were initially skeptical of Macpherson's design. As Macpherson wrote: "They all thought it impractical—thought a man would smother in it. I assured them I knew he would not and a Colonel Harvey, R.E., put it on and went into the stink chamber and we turned on the gas. After about 5 minutes he walked toward the door pulling off the helmet as he came. I pulled open the door and threw a spray of the hypo solution over him calling him to run out. He was coming to ask us what we were waiting for. Why did we not turn on the Chlorine? He was surprised when we told him he had been in a concentration of Chlorine 10 times as strong as the Germans could get over to our trenches."

The British War Office was impressed and put Macpherson in charge of manufacturing the gas mask. "The work soon outgrew the Factory as far as anything but the cutting and sewing of the helmets was concerned and we took over three of the biggest laundries in London for the dipping and parcelling," wrote Macpherson. "To do this work I sent out a call for women volunteers. I soon had hundreds from all classes of society. Only the fore-women were paid and I had three 8-hour shifts working in each laundry."

Cluny Macpherson (standing centre) with members of the Newfoundland Regiment's Ambulance Unit.
The Rooms Provincial Archives Division, A 27-17

Gas masks were made for horses too.
The War of the Nations *(New York: New York Times, Co., 1919)*

In the coming months, Macpherson and his colleagues continued to modify the design. The eyepiece was improved and a mouthpiece added. Scientists also found ways to block a wider range of dangerous chemicals.

"And so, while the production of the helmet went ahead full speed, we were busy devising the box respirator, in which, by drawing the breath through a can of powdered carbon, gases for which there was no practical chemical antidote could be absorbed," Macpherson continued. "The devising and making of these—the fore-runner of the respirators of to-day—was a slow business, and my helmets were made to the number of over 22 millions."

Macpherson's team had just gotten the box-respirator ready for production when he was ordered to Gallipoli in July 1915. Allied commanders were worried that the Turkish Army was planning a gas attack and they wanted Macpherson to teach officers how to use the helmet.

Although his instructions saved countless lives, Macpherson himself fell ill with dysentery during his visit to the front lines and he spent much of November hospitalized. When he returned to active duty, he was ordered to Italy, and then Egypt, but was again admitted to hospital on February 3, 1916, after his horse stumbled and threw him to the ground. Macpherson's foot was fractured and he suffered internal injuries.

Macpherson's health never returned to what it was before Gallipoli: breathlessness, heart trouble, and swollen ankles were recurring problems. In October, military doctors ordered him back to Newfoundland.

A Hero of the Ambulance Unit

When war broke out on August 4, 1914, many members of the St. John Ambulance Brigade volunteered for the Newfoundland Regiment's Ambulance Unit. Their job was to deliver emergency medical care on the front lines. It was dangerous work and many died in the line of duty.

One of the first fatalities in the New-foundland Regiment's Ambulance Unit was Private John Fitzgerald. He was shot dead while trying to attend to another man's wounds on the battlefield at Gallipoli on December 1, 1915.

Governor Sir Walter Davidson later praised Fitzgerald's actions in a public notice: "The gallantry of this Newfoundland Soldier is well known to all who live in the Colony. He belonged to the Ambulance Section and laid down his life while binding up the wounds of others under enemy fire outside the trenches at Suvla Bay on the Gallipoli Peninsula on December 1st 1915."

John Fitzgerald was 31 when he died.

Left to right: Pts. Michael O'Neill, Charles Parsons, and Alfred Taylor. All three died at Beaumont-Hamel on July 1, 1916.
The Rooms Provincial Archives Division, E-29-56, E-17-3, E-17-7

five casualties when German bullets wounded four men and killed 19-year-old Private George Curnew. More casualties followed in the coming weeks.

As the date of the battle approached, the men of the Newfoundland Regiment grew apprehensive. "There seems to be a strange pensiveness about everything and we are all strangely thoughtful about the 'Great Push'," Lieutenant Owen Steele wrote in his diary on June 20.

Yet Steele also expressed a confidence in the strength of the Allied forces and found comfort in a shared sense of purpose and duty. "Everyone seems so cool about it all, quietly preparing for what is going to be the greatest attack in the history of the world, and very possibly the greatest there will ever be,"

O f all the battles the Newfoundland Regiment fought during World War I, none was as devastating or as defining as the first day of the Battle of the Somme. The Regiment's tragic advance at Beaumont-Hamel on the morning of July 1, 1916, became an enduring symbol of its valour and its terrible wartime sacrifices. The events of that day were forever seared into the cultural memory of Newfoundlanders and Labradorians.

At the start of 1916, the Allied forces were in trouble. The Gallipoli Campaign had been a failure. The Eastern Front was in disarray and the Western Front was locked in a stalemate. Germany had marched through Belgium and into northern France, where its army was securely entrenched near the River Somme. British and French forces desperately needed a success. Commanders spent the winter planning a major offensive to regain control of the Somme.

Their plans were upset when Germany launched a massive attack against French forces near Verdun (a city in northeast France) on February 21, 1916. The battle lasted for almost 10 months and monopolized many of the French troops originally intended for the Somme offensive. As a result, Britain had to divert many of its troops to the Somme, and the battle became primarily a British operation.

The Newfoundland Regiment, still with the 88th Brigade of the 29th Division, received word on February 25, 1916, that it would be part of the Somme offensive. It departed Egypt on March 14, 1916, and arrived in France eight days later. For the next three months, it readied for combat. The men trained rigorously, did tours of duty on the front line, dug trenches, strengthened defences, and observed the enemy.

Although the battle would not begin until July 1, the months leading up to it were dangerous. The Germans often shelled Allied trenches, and snipers were another threat. On April 24, the Regiment sustained

Newfoundland soldiers in the support trench nicknamed St. John's Road before their attack at Beaumont-Hamel.
The Rooms Provincial Archives Division, NA 3105

24

he wrote on June 23. "We only hope that it may be a very strong factor in bringing an early end to the war."

Many soldiers sent reassuring letters home in the days leading up to the battle, although censorship laws prohibited them from revealing the Allies' plans. "This letter will be very short for we have been up to our eyes in work for the past fortnight and will be for some time to come, the reason for which I cannot give you even an inkling; but you will have heard all before this reaches you," Steele wrote to his parents on June 25.

"Am afraid that quite a long time will elapse before you get another letter from us, but you need not worry for we shall be all right. Jim [Steele's brother] and I are both OK and in the best of spirits, and I hope it will *not* be long before we shall be *able* to write you a decent letter *each*.... Am hoping that there will be a possibility of our spending Christmas with you all this year. Would not that be grand!"

Private Lind's letter to the *Daily News* on June 29 was filled with bravado, which masked any anxiety he may have felt: "No pen could describe what it is like, how calmly one stands and faces death, jokes and laughs; everything is just an every day occurrence. You are mud covered, dry and caked, perhaps, but you look at the chap next you and laugh at the state he is in; then you look down at your own clothes and then the other fellow laughs. Then a whizz bang comes across and misses both of you, and both laugh together."

From the Diary of Owen Steele
June 20, 1916

Today has been a moderately quiet day. The Germans' gifts today, in the way of shells, amounted to only 70, but we had four men wounded, one of whom may die, for the main artery of one of his legs has been severed; he is an Assyrian named Joe Sheehan. One of the men wounded yesterday has since died, also a man who met with a bomb accident, a piece going into his eye and probably touching a portion of his brain. There seems to be a strange pensiveness about everything and we are all strangely thoughtful about the "Great Push."

June 21, 1916

The Huns certainly appear to be expecting our visit, for they are, according to reports, all along the front, hard at work. There is an immense amount of traffic everywhere. Opposite our particular position, they are seen working by day and night—with great care of course, and there is quite a lot of traffic. Only last night, they could be heard strengthening their wire work and even adding to it. Then their aeroplanes are busy all day seeking information, by flying over our lines.

Newfoundland Regiment soldiers, n.d. *The Rooms Provincial Archives Division, F 37-24*

On June 24, the Allied powers bombarded the German front lines with artillery. The barrage, which lasted for a week, was intended to weaken enemy defences in advance of the July 1 ground attack.

At 9 p.m. on June 30, the Regiment departed Louvencourt and marched three hours to its trenches on the battlefield. "It is surprising to see how happy and light-hearted everyone is, and yet this is undoubtedly the last day for a good many," Steele wrote in his diary.

"The various Battalions marched off whistling and singing and it was a great sight. Of course, this is the best way to take things and hope for the best."

The Danger Tree is preserved at the Beaumont-Hamel Newfoundland Memorial that opened in 1925. *ASC, Coll. 308 1.25.010*

The Battle of the Somme took place on a 30-kilometre front near the River Somme in northern France. Allied trenches stretched along one side and the Germans along the other. In between lay No Man's Land.

The Newfoundland Regiment's assignment (along with the rest of the 88th Brigade's) was to seize control of the German trenches near the village of Beaumont-Hamel. It was a difficult task. The German lines were about 300 to 500 metres away, down a grassy slope, and behind thick entanglements of barbed wire—it was one of the best fortified positions on the entire battlefield.

The offensive began on the morning of July 1, 1916. At 6 a.m., Allied forces bombarded the Germans with artillery for about an hour. At 7:20 a.m., they detonated more than 18,000 kilograms of explosives under Hawthorn Ridge, an important German stronghold on its front line, about 700 metres to the west of Beaumont-Hamel. The blast turned the area into a giant crater measuring 40 metres wide and 18 metres deep.

In the preceding weeks, Allied commanders had debated whether to detonate the explosives four hours before the ground attack, two minutes before the attack, or at the very moment the soldiers left their trenches. A compromise placed the detonation at 10 minutes before zero hour. The timing was a terrible mistake. The explosion alerted Germans that a land attack was imminent, while the 10-minute delay gave them just enough time to strengthen their defences and ready their machine guns.

As the first wave of Allied troops left their trenches at 7:30 a.m., they were greeted by a devastating barrage of enemy artillery and machine-gun fire, stronger than anyone had anticipated. Most men were killed or wounded in minutes. A second wave of troops left their trenches soon after and met the same fate. The Newfoundland Regiment was still in its trenches, awaiting orders to go over the top as part of a third wave of attack.

By 8 a.m., there was considerable confusion along the Allied lines. Although the first two waves of attack had failed, British commanders were receiving conflicting reports from the battlefield. Making matters even worse, divisional commanders mistook German flares for a signal of success from Britain's 87th Brigade. At 8:45 a.m., Brigadier General Douglas Edward Cayley ordered the Newfoundland Regiment to advance "as soon as possible."

The men left their trenches at 9:15 a.m., with orders to seize the first and second lines of enemy trenches. But as they moved out of their own front lines, no friendly fire covered their advance and German shells killed or wounded most of the men before they even reached No Man's Land.

Private Anthony Stacey described the advance in his *Memoirs of a Blue Puttee*: "the wire had been cut in our front line and bridges laid across the trench the night before. This was a death trap for our boys as the enemy just set the sights of their machine guns on the gaps in the barbed wire and fired."

Commanders made another terrible error in judgment by ordering the men to wear shiny tin triangles on their backs. The hope was that the triangles would help Allied aircraft identify their men, but instead they provided the German snipers with excellent targets.

There were other flaws in the Allied strategy. The week-long bombardment that preceded the attack did not weaken German defences as much as Allied commanders had hoped, but

A Dangerous Retreat

After the attack ended on the morning of July 1, 1916, survivors still trapped in No Man's Land spent hours, and in some cases days, trying to return to their own lines without getting killed by enemy snipers. Private James McGrath lay on the battlefield for about 17 hours before he finally made it to safety. He described his ordeal to the *Newfoundland Quarterly* in its fall 1916 edition:

"The Germans actually mowed us down like sheep. I managed to get to their barbed wire, where I got the first shot; then went to jump into their trench when I got the second in the leg. I lay in No Man's Land for fifteen hours, and then crawled a distance of a mile and a quarter. They fired on me again, this time fetching me in the left leg, and so I waited for another hour and moved again, only having the use of my left arm now. As I was doing splendidly, nearing our own trench they again fetched me, this time around the hip as I crawled on. I managed to get to our own line which I saw was evacuated as our artillery was playing heavily on their trenches. They retaliated and kept me in a hole for another hour. I was then rescued by Captain Windeler who took me on his back to the dressing station a distance of two miles. Well, thank God my wounds are all flesh wounds and won't take long to heal up."

Five of the Newfoundlanders killed at Beaumont-Hamel on July 1, 1916.

Michael Walsh

William Morgan

William White

Frederick Snow

Allan Lyons

it did have the unanticipated effect of destroying almost every tree, shrub, and ridge that once covered No Man's Land and could have offered the advancing Allied soldiers life-saving cover from enemy fire.

One survivor of the bombardment was the trunk of a blasted apple tree, which stood about halfway down the slope between the British and German trenches. Now known as the Danger Tree, it became a rallying point for the men of the Newfoundland Regiment who had made it into No Man's Land. But the tree provided meagre cover, and the men became silhouetted against the sky as they approached it, making them easy targets for German gunners. Many soldiers died near the Danger Tree, including Private Lind. He was 37.

The few men who reached the enemy lines made a terrible discovery: the week-long artillery bombardment that preceded their advance had not severed the German barbed wire as expected. Instead, it remained intact—a formidable defence against invaders.

Frustratingly, Allied leaders had already obtained this information from reconnaissance teams who had visited the German lines in the nights leading up to the attack, but they had dismissed the reports, convinced that the scouts were inexperienced and the artillery barrage much more effective than it actually was. Many of the soldiers who reached the enemy lines died there, trapped in the uncut wire.

At 9:45 a.m., the Regiment's commanding officer, Lieutenant Colonel Arthur Hadow, reported to headquarters that the attack had failed. The outcome was devastating. In a single morning, almost 20,000 British troops died, and another 37,000 were wounded. The Newfoundland Regiment had been almost wiped out. When roll call was taken, only 68 men answered their names: 324 were killed, or missing and presumed dead, and 386 were wounded.

27

THE HOME FRONT REACTS

When news of Beaumont-Hamel reached Newfoundland and Labrador, it plunged the dominion into widespread mourning. Casualty lists appeared in local newspapers and post offices, but information, often incomplete, came in slowly from the front lines. Many families had to endure a few tortuous weeks of wondering whether their loved ones were alive or dead.

Opening of the Newfoundland Beaumont-Hamel Memorial, June 7, 1925. *The Rooms Provincial Archives Division, NA 3106*

Among them was Emilie Florence Knight, whose son, William, was a sergeant in the Newfoundland Regiment. She wrote to him on July 18, desperate for news:

My dear Will,
    I was in great trouble for a time, after that battle. I was expecting to see your number. Oh! It was dreadful, ten times worse than it really was and it was bad enough. I thought of you when you told me always to remember (no news is good news). I didn't eat anything for days ... Poor grandpa is like a fish out of water, he got the post-office steps worn down going up to see the names.
From your loving Mother

William's grandfather also wrote a letter:

My dear Willie,
    I am writing you these few lines to let you know that I got your letter of the 18th of June in due time and we were very glad to hear you were in good health when you wrote, and I hope this will find [you] the same now.
    But I see by the papers that you fought a big battle since then and I hope to God you came through it alright, for it must have been an awful time, and if you got through you must be one of the very lucky ones. I only hope you did, and if you did, we must thank god for it. If I can judge from the number of killed and wounded on the casualties list that have come in, they number up to now over 500 and are still coming in. But you are not among the number that have come in so far and I hope and pray to God you won't be on it.
    From ever loving Grandpa Warren

Sergeant William Knight was killed at Beaumont-Hamel on July 1, 1916. He was 23.

After William Knight was killed on July 1, 1916, letters from his mother and grandfather were returned, unopened, in envelopes with the word "Dead" written across them in red ink.

The days after Beaumont-Hamel brought more death. Lieutenant Steele had survived the offence only to be hit by a German shell on July 7 just outside his lodgings. He died one day later.

British officers sent letters of condolence to the many families who had lost sons, husbands, fathers, and brothers, and Allied leaders publicly praised the Newfoundland Regiment. Among them was Sir Douglas Haig, Commander-in-Chief of the British Forces. "Newfoundland may well feel proud of her sons," the *Evening Telegram* quoted him as saying on July 21, 1916: "The heroism and devotion to duty they displayed on the first July has never been surpassed. Please convey my deepest sympathy, and that of the whole of our armies in France in the loss of the brave officers and men who have fallen for the Empire, and our admiration of their heroic conduct. Their efforts contributed to our success, and their example will live."

Praise also came from Sir Aylmer Hunter-Weston, the General Commanding Officer of the 29th Division of the British Army. "Newfoundlanders, I salute you individually," he said. "You have done better than the best."

The Battle of Beaumont-Hamel had far-reaching effects in Newfoundland and Labrador. The first Memorial Day ceremony took place in downtown St. John's one year later. In the 1920s, the government bought the ground on which the Newfoundland Regiment fought. The memorial park it established at Beaumont-Hamel became a place of pilgrimage for people wishing to honour and mourn the Regiment.

July 1 remains an official day of remembrance in Newfoundland and Labrador. People gather annually at the National War Memorial in downtown St. John's and at other locations across the province or in Europe to remember those sol-

A sketch of the Newfoundland Regiment at Beaumont-Hamel. *The Veteran* 5.3 *(1926)*

diers who fought at Beaumont-Hamel, as well as the many other men and women who have served in other forces and other wars.

---

febiruary 20th 1922

Lieut-Col t Mangle

Dear sir i ham only a lettel Boy not quit seven yars old i go to school Every Day and i ham in no, one Book and i keep hed of the Class Every Day and i had one Dollar gave me four keeping hed of the Class so i ham sending it to you four Bhaumont hamel memorial that is the spot ware my Fathare was kelled july the First 1916

i ham in Closing one Dollar .

yours Very truly

Harry White

Twillingate Dunrells arm

sir if you got Eny Fishear Books to spare Pa send me some to look at some times i ham Very fond of Books

A Great Mistake

On February 20, 1922, a little boy named Harry White donated one dollar to a fundraising campaign to create a Beaumont-Hamel memorial. "[T]hat is the spot ware my Fathare was kelled july the First 1916," he wrote.

Harry never had the chance to meet his father. Frederick White of Durrell's Arm went off to war before his son was born. His letters home are filled with regret and sadness. "If I comes home from the war safe I will marry you," he wrote to his sweetheart on September 2, 1916, from a training camp in Scotland.

He wrote again on September 20: "I know now I made a great mistake, Mary, to go away and leave you like you was. I shall always have it on my mind as long as I lives."

Frederick White was 24 when he was killed at Beaumont-Hamel.

The St. John's Daily Star

Newfoundland

| VOLUME II. | ($3.00 per Annum.) | MONDAY, JULY 10, 1916. | (Price: One Cent.) | No. 159. |

GENERAL HAIG PRAISES HEROISM AND DEVOTION OF NEWFOUNDLANDERS

(No. 330. Telegram, received 9th July, 7.30 p.m.)

To Governor. Newfoundland:

Newfoundland may well feel proud of her sons. The heroism and devotion to duty they displayed on 1st July has never been surpassed. Please convey my deep sympathy and that of the whole of our armies in France in the loss of the brave officers and men who have fallen for the Empire, and our admiration of their heroic conduct. Their efforts contributed to our success, and their example will live.
— DOUGLAS HAIG, Field Marshal.

The Soldiers of Newfoundland have won the highest praise which a Son of Britain can ever earn.

The Glory of it can never fade. The First of July when our heroes fought and fell, will stand for ever as the proudest day in the history of the Loyal Colony.
— THE GOVERNOR

July 9th, 1916.

The Battle of Beaumont-Hamel had decimated the Newfoundland Regiment. Almost every survivor had lost someone in the attack—a brother, a cousin, a close friend. It took them five days to bury their dead, then it was time to regroup and rebuild.

A draft of 127 reinforcements arrived on July 11, which brought the unit up to 11 officers and 271 other ranks. More drafts followed, but it was a slow process and the Regiment would not number 800 men again until December 1916.

In the meantime, the Regiment alternated between serving on the front lines and in reserve positions. From July 14 to 17, 1916, it did a brief tour of duty on the front lines near Auchonvillers, about 2 kilometres west of Beaumont-Hamel. It then spent two months at Ypres, Belgium, where it dug and repaired trenches and accepted additional drafts of new recruits.

A. Rice, George Mullett, and Newman Gough.
ASC, Coll. 346 1.01.051.

While at Ypres, the Regiment came under its first attack by German poison gas on August 8. Fortunately, the soldiers were equipped with gas masks—which the Regiment's own Major Cluny Macpherson had helped to invent—and survived the assault without a single casualty.

On October 5, 1916, the Regiment departed Belgium for northern France. The Battle of the Somme, which had begun on July 1, was still not over, and Allied leaders once again needed the Newfoundland Regiment on the front lines, this time near the village of Gueudecourt, about 16 kilometres east of Beaumont-Hamel. Its assignment was to take possession of Hilt Trench, a German stronghold, which lay just 400 metres from the British front lines.

The attack began at precisely 2:05 p.m. on October 12, 1916. As the Newfoundland soldiers left their trenches, they encountered a devastating barrage

A Soldier's Uniform

A soldier in the Newfoundland Regiment went to war in wool. Their jackets (called tunics) and trousers were made from thick khaki wool, and their shirts from a lighter wool flannel. The men wound khaki wool puttees around their lower legs and wore brown leather boots, equipped with hobnails and heel cleats. The tunics had four brass buttons and four outside pockets. It was not unusual for a soldier to carry a pay book, bible, cigarette case, and letters from home in the pocket over his heart. There was also one inside pocket, which held the field dressing.

There was a variety of headgear. Service dress caps featured a stiff peak that jutted out below a brown leather strap. From 1916 on, some soldiers were also issued a less formal soft trench hat. It was similar in appearance to the dress cap, but could be rolled up and stuffed into backpacks. There was also the steel combat helmet, which was worn at the front, both in battle and as part of everyday life in the trenches.

The outfit varied somewhat with the climate and location. In warmer places, like Egypt, the troops wore uniforms made from a lighter material, known as khaki drill. They covered

their heads with lightweight sun helmets (also known as pith or safari helmets), which were designed to shade the face from the sun. In colder climates, the men wore thick overcoats and knit caps.

When the men were in the trenches or on the battlefield, they often carried a lot of equipment. This could include a canteen, trench lantern, trench club, bayonet, rifle, ammunition, grenades, shovel, identification tags, field dressing, and gas mask. Soldiers also carried personal items inside a shoulder bag. These typically included a fork and knife, mug, shaving kit, and food rations.

of enemy fire. Captain Bertram Butler later wrote about the offensive for *The Veteran* in June 1922:

"Although our attack was only on a front of about three hundred yards, it was impossible for one who took part in it to see what went on, except in his immediate vicinity. One platoon of B Company was practically wiped out, but the one on its right hardly had a casualty until we reached the German line. A Company had extremely hard luck, losing all its officers before they were nearly across; the non-commissioned officers took up the commands, however, and pushed the attack home. All ranks were eager to avenge as far as possible our comrades who fell on July first."

When the Regiment finally made it to Hilt Trench, they had to engage in close-range combat with the Germans—young men who

Almost one year after he had helped capture Caribou Hill at Gallipoli, James Donnelly was killed in action at Gueudecourt.

were just as scared as they were. Many of the Newfoundlanders had not used their bayonets outside of training exercises, but they prevailed despite their inexperience—by 2:30 p.m., the Germans had surrendered and the Newfoundland Regiment was in control of Hilt Trench.

It was an important victory, but it came at a terrible cost: 120 of the Regiment's men were killed and 119 wounded. About 250 Germans died and another 150 were taken prisoners. The Newfoundland Regiment maintained control of Hilt Trench until 3 a.m. the following morning, when another Allied unit arrived to relieve it. The men marched back to Gueudecourt for much-needed food and sleep. Their last major involvement in the Battle of the Somme was over.

LCpl. Chesley Gough, 23, was killed by an enemy shell at Gueudecourt.

LCpl. Hardy Frederic Snow, 21, died in the same battle.

The Trench System

A complex network of trenches snaked across the Western Front. It began at the Belgian coast, stretched through northeast France, and ended at the Swiss border. The Allied forces usually dug a series of three parallel trenches. The first, the front (or firing) line, guarded by barbed wire, lay next to No Man's Land, which separated the Allied and German trenches. No Man's Land could be 50 metres to 1.5 kilometres wide.

A few hundred metres to the rear of the front line was a support trench filled with men and supplies ready to assist the front-line soldiers. Farther back was a reserve trench containing additional men and supplies. Smaller communication trenches connected the three main trenches and allowed for the movement of men, messages, and supplies between the front-line, support, and reserve trenches.

Rather than run in straight lines, these three trenches followed a zigzag route, which made it easier to evade enemy fire. It has been estimated that if all the trenches were laid end to end, they would extend for about 40,200 kilometres, of which about 19,000 kilometres belonged to the Allies.

Monchy-le-Preux, 1917

The Battle of Monchy.

Capt. Rev. Fr. Nangle, C. F., Gives Thrilling Description of the Fight — Defeat Turned to Victory by Gallantry of 'Ours.'

(From the Daily News)

Newfoundland Regiment at Berneville after fighting at Monchy-le-Preux, April 1917. *The Rooms Provincial Archives Division, VA 157-9*

Sable Chief

Around the same time the Monchy Ten were battling Germans, an unusual new recruit arrived at the Newfoundland Regiment's depot at Ayr, Scotland. Sable Chief was a 200-pound Newfoundland dog who became the Regiment's much-loved mascot. He was trained to march in formation and stand at attention when the Regimental Band played "God Save the King." Sable even went on a brief tour of England with the Band in 1917, and postcards bearing his image became a popular item for soldiers to send home. Sable Chief died in 1918 after he was accidentally hit by a truck. His body was sent to a taxidermist and is held at The Rooms Provincial Museum in St. John's.

After its engagement at Gueudecourt in October 1916, the Newfoundland Regiment spent a few months alternating between the front lines, reserve trenches, and rest camps.

On January 27, 1917, it took part in a surprise attack against the Germans near the village of Le Transloy in northern France. The battle was a victory for the British forces, who took 368 German prisoners, including 72 captured by the Newfoundland Regiment's Sergeant Major Cyril Gardner. As a result of his actions, Gardner received a Bar to the Distinguished Conduct Medal which he had previously earned at Gueudecourt.

The Regiment took part in another battle from March 2 to 3, 1917, this time near the French village of Sailly-Saillisel. Temporarily attached to the British 86th Brigade, it helped to fend off attacking Germans and capture enemy trenches. Although the operation was a success, the Regiment lost 71 soldiers: 27 killed and 44 wounded.

Its next major engagement was in the Battle of Arras. On April 11, 1917, British forces seized the French village of Monchy-le-Preux from German control. The Newfoundland Regiment was part of a subsequent plan to drive German forces from the surrounding land.

Allied commanders ordered the 88th Brigade, which included the Newfoundland and Essex Regiments, to capture a German trench located just east of Monchy-le-Preux, and then secure Infantry Hill, which lay about 900 metres outside the village. The hill was strategically important because of the extensive view it provided of the region.

Zero hour was set for 5:30 a.m. on April 14, 1917. Within two hours, the Regiment had captured both of its objectives and with only a relatively small number of casualties. However, the Germans launched a fierce counterattack, which cut off the Newfoundland Regiment's C and D Companies from the rest of the Allied troops. Surrounded and greatly outnumbered, the men sustained heavy casualties and were forced to surrender.

At Battalion Headquarters, the Newfoundland Regiment's commanding officer, Lieutenant-Colonel James Forbes-Robertson, ordered a scout to go forward and observe the situation. He returned with upsetting news: not a single unwounded man from the Newfoundland Regiment existed east of Monchy-le-Preux and about 200 or 300 German troops

All that stood between Monchy-le-Preux and the more than 200 advancing Germans were nine Newfoundlanders and one soldier from the Essex Regiment. Among them was Private Fred Curran, who later wrote about that day for *The Veteran*:

"We opened fire on the Germans immediately and, I suppose, we successfully created the delusion that we were a large invincible army, because they made no strong attack. Then suddenly, our ammunition gave out. On no man's land were machine gun carriers lying among the dead men and debris, and we got enough ammunition to keep up a continuous firing for over an hour."

By the time reinforcements arrived at 8 p.m., the village had been saved and those who protected it became forever known as the Monchy Ten. Allied commanders later estimated that if the Germans had captured the village, it would have taken about 40,000 troops to reclaim it.

After Monchy-le-Preux, the Regiment was involved in one more operation at Arras. On April 23, it helped to guard a portion of the front line on the Arras-Cambrai road immediately south of Monchy. The area came under intense enemy fire and an already depleted Newfoundland Regiment sustained further casualties: 13 killed and 48 wounded.

The nine Newfoundlanders who saved Monchy-le-Preux. Back row, left to right: Cpl. Albert S. Rose; Sgt. Walter Pitcher; Lt.-Col. James Forbes-Robertson; Lieut. Kevin M. Keegan; Sgt. Charles Parsons; Sgt. Joseph R. Waterfield. Front row, left to right: Pte. Frederick Curran; Cpl. John Hillier; Pte. Japheth Hounsell. *The Rooms Provincial Archives Division, VA 157-11*

were advancing toward the village. Losing control of Monchy-le-Preux would be a devastating loss for the Allies.

Forbes-Robertson quickly gathered 21 soldiers from the Newfoundland and Essex Regiments who were still able to fight and led them to a trench near the edge of town, where they stood the best chance of holding off the Germans until reinforcements arrived.

To reach the trench the Regiment would first have to cross about 100 metres of open ground, in full sight of the Germans. They made their advance under a hail of enemy fire; only nine reached their target—eight from the Newfoundland Regiment and one from the Essex Regiment. They were later joined by a tenth soldier, John Hillier of St. John's, who had been struck by a bursting shell that had rendered him temporarily unconscious. They opened fire on the Germans at about 10:50 a.m.

Fred Curran Remembers Monchy-le-Preux

"On the next day—the 12th—we marched to Arras. As we marched along the main road from Gouy-en-Artois, the landscape became more and more desolate. Gradually, we were entering the war-swept territory. Under the grey, ominous sky, the bared farms, bereft of their hedges and fruit trees with their dilapidated, deserted cottages, presented a spectacle as sad and depressing as one could witness.

"Just as we entered the town an incendiary shell struck the spire of the church. It crashed and fell, its ruins blocking our way. The church caught fire and kept burning all night long. The noise was indescribable. The shrieking of a shell is bad enough in all conscience, when it bursts in an open field, but it becomes intensified a hundred times when it bursts in the narrow streets between stone houses.

"Our objective was Infantry Hill and just as our men reached it, the Germans swarmed over in incredible numbers. Already their shellfire had depleted our ranks tremendously. The result was inevitable. At nine in the morning a runner from the battalion reported the Germans were coming towards Monchy in extended order and that our battalion had been completely wiped out.

"We had been in the trench for ten hours and six of us remained to hand over our position to the company. We immediately went back to battalion headquarters in the town, guided—as much as by anything—by the dull glare of the burning church. When we called the roll that evening there were twenty-five survivors to return to our ten percent reserve."

After the Battle of Arras, the Newfound-land Regiment entered a well-deserved period of rest and recuperation before returning to the front lines later that summer. It fought at Belgium in July 1917, and again in September and October. In November, it returned to France to take part in the Battle of Cambrai.

By then, war tactics were changing. The Germans were using mustard gas with greater regularity and tanks were becoming more common on the battleground. At the Battle of Cambrai, Allied forces used about 100 tanks and the Newfoundland Regiment had to train for weeks to learn how to advance on foot behind the large machines.

The Allies launched their surprise attack on November 20, 1917. Cambrai was an important supply point for German troops, and Allied commanders hoped to capture it from enemy control. But to reach the area, troops first had to fight their way through 10 kilometres of German-controlled territory.

The Newfoundland Regiment's assignment was to advance behind the first waves of attackers and capture the St. Quentin Canal and the town of Masnières. Other Allied troops would follow and push on to Cambrai.

Newfoundland soldiers possibly washing boards which might be used for temporary shelter.
The Rooms Provincial Archives Division, VA 40-21.3

Boys on the Battlefield

On October 9, 1917, the Newfoundland Regiment took part in the Battle of Poelcappelle, in Belgium. Its job was to help advance the Allied line about 2,000 yards north and push back the Germans. Although the Regiment initially reached its objective, it had to fall back 200 yards after the Germans blasted them with heavy artillery and sniper fire. As well as losing ground, lives were lost—48 died that day, another 127 were wounded.

Among the dead was a 17-year-old soldier. Leo Christopher had reported that he was 18 years old when he had joined the Regiment two years earlier. He was one of the many underage soldiers who had slipped past recruiters and into the Regiment. It was an easy accomplishment. Recruiters were desperate for soldiers and did not ask for a formal proof of age. If they did discover that a volunteer was underage, then a letter of permission from a parent or guardian was often all that was needed to send a boy to war.

If the underage soldier was not discovered before going overseas, parents were sometimes powerless to remove their sons from the trenches. On June 1, 1917, Leo's mother, Kate, wrote Governor Sir Edward Davidson, imploring him to grant her son temporary leave.

Kate Christopher was never reunited with her son. He was reported missing on October 9, 1917, and was later presumed dead. Christopher was one of the approximately 272 underage Newfoundland Regiment soldiers who are believed to have died in the war.

The Newfoundland Regiment had secured its first objective by 1:30 p.m. and then proceeded to Masnières. It fought all night to rid the town of German troops; by morning it was almost entirely under Allied control. Reinforcements relieved the Regiment at 2 a.m. on November 22. The success did not come easily—54 of the Regiment died in the two-day attack, and 188 more were wounded.

The Regiment had little time to rest before the Germans launched a powerful counterattack on November 30. The fighting lasted for days. Soldiers engaged in hand-to-hand combat and they were shelled repeatedly. Approximately 50 Newfoundlanders and Labradorians died before the Regiment withdrew at 9 p.m. on December 3; about 200 were wounded or taken prisoner. The survivors proceeded to a rest camp at Humbercourt.

Newfoundland soldiers near Hesdin, 20 December 1917. *Imperial War Museums, Q 8353*

By then, the Newfoundland Regiment had gained a reputation for courage and tenacity. It had fought with distinction in several major battles and many of its members had earned medals for their acts of bravery. On December 17, 1917, King George V honoured the entire Regiment by bestowing the title of *Royal* to the unit. It was an award that no other British Regiment earned during the war. It gave both the Regiment and the dominion of Newfoundland a much-needed morale boost as 1917 came to a close.

Life in the Trenches

Soldiers lived for weeks in the trenches. Each battalion was expected to serve in the front-line trenches, followed by a tour in the support and reserve trenches, before being granted a short period of rest. The cycle was then repeated. The precise amount of time the men spent in the trenches varied enormously, depending on the intensity of combat, the availability of reserve troops, and even the weather. In the early stages of war, the men generally spent four days on the front lines, four in the reserve trenches, and four at rest. But as hostilities intensified, front-line duty lengthened considerably, as recruiting became a problem.

Life in the trenches was dirty, dangerous, and monotonous. The daily routine began about an hour before sunrise, when all front-line soldiers had to stand on guard with rifles and bayonets ready for a possible early-morning enemy attack. This was known as the "stand-to." By 7 a.m. it was sufficiently light to end the stand-to and have breakfast. Then the officers inspected the soldiers and assigned them daily chores, which might include repairing trench floors, refilling sandbags on top of trench walls, or (most dreaded) emptying the latrines. The men also took turns being on watch against enemy attack.

Major attacks, however, were rare and much of the men's time in the front-line trenches was marked by monotonous routine. Enemy snipers made it impossible for soldiers to move about much in the daylight, so their actions were severely limited. During the daytime the front-line soldier had the most time to rest, and he used the quiet hours to write letters home, play cards, or catch a few hours of much-needed sleep.

Just before dusk, the soldiers once again had to stand-to. After nightfall, they became active. Darkness afforded them enough safety to venture out and perform a variety of tasks—repairing barbed wire, digging trenches, fetching supplies from the rear lines, and patrolling No Man's Land.

Disease was a significant threat on the front lines. The trenches were impossible to keep clean. Latrines often overflowed and the men had to go days or even weeks without a proper bath. Rain could turn the trenches into a grimy hellhole. Adding to the horror were the hundreds and sometimes thousands of rotting bodies of soldiers that littered No Man's Land or were buried in shallow graves. Stench was a daily part of life, and so were rats and lice. Disease and infection became a recurring problem and a severe threat to every soldier's health.

One of the most notorious afflictions was trench foot. After prolonged exposure to the wet, cold, and unsanitary conditions of the trench floors, the skin on a man's foot died and turned black or white. Amputation was often the only treatment.

While the Newfoundland Regiment was fighting overseas, political battles were being waged back home. A series of controversies developed in 1916 and 1917 that undermined the public's confidence in the government and eventually led to a change in administration and the dismantling of the Newfoundland Patriotic Association.

By 1917, low enlistment rates had damaged the NPA's credibility. As the hopes of a short war dwindled, so did the supply of volunteers. The staggering losses that the Regiment had sustained at Beaumont-Hamel and subsequent battles made recruitment even more challenging. It soon became impossible for the NPA to find enough new volunteers to keep pace with casualties.

Other problems also plagued the NPA. When wounded soldiers returned home in 1916, no effective military pension or work-placement programs awaited them. These men publicly criticized the NPA and some local newspapers called upon the government to step in.

Dissatisfaction surrounding the selection of Regiment officers was another issue. Critics accused the NPA of awarding too many commissions to St. John's residents, Protestants, and the social elite, and too few to outport residents, Catholics, and soldiers from the working class.

On November 30, 1917, the St. John's *Daily Star* published a letter from an anonymous soldier who was upset about the unfair situation: "There are able-bodied young men attached to the base and headquarters in Scotland, who should be in the trenches in France, relieving the men who have borne the heat and burden of the fray during the whole course of the war. They are there who have never been any nearer than Ayr to the firing line, who are enjoying the time of their lives,

The Newfoundland Regiment marching in St. John's before going overseas, 1915.
The Rooms Provincial Archives Division, VA 37-17.1

in comfortable quarters, drawing pay as privates, corporals, sergeants, lieutenants and captains, the majority of them in much better physical condition for the firing line than many of the long-service men now there."

Even more damaging were accusations that some of the NPA's own members were abusing their positions to profit financially from the war. It involved shipping. The Newfoundland economy relied on the import and export of goods, but in 1915 some local merchant firms sold their largest icebreakers to Russia so it could safeguard its northern waters.

It was an opportune time for the merchants, because the ships were costly to maintain, but their sale decreased the number of local vessels available to import goods like flour, coal, and salt to Newfoundland and Labrador. Shortages of these and other commodities followed, and prices rose.

Rumours that the merchants were also abusing their influence over the local market to obtain the highest possible margin of profit soon spread. Some of the men implicated were NPA members.

William Coaker, leader of the Union Party, became one of the more vocal critics of what he called the profiteering merchants. "If the public knew the one half of what is going on in official circles the past few months, they would stand appalled," he wrote in the *Mail and Advocate* on March 1, 1916. "They have been asked to contribute to collections for patriotic purposes. They have been asked to make many sacrifices which they have done with true British spirit. But in return for all this they find themselves at the mercy of a ring of commercial grafters."

The press was also critical. In February 1916, the *Evening Telegram* ran a series of editorials calling the government to action.

William Coaker with the members of the Union Party in 1919, was a vocal opponent to both the NPA and the "profiteering merchants" during the war. *The Rooms Provincial Archives Division, VA 82-20.2*

It suggested that the dominion fix freight rates and introduce an excess profits tax to past and future sales, the proceeds of which could go to the war effort. The *Daily News* criticized merchants in an editorial on March 16, 1916, claiming that they engaged in "the kind of patriotism that pays."

In May 1917, Prime Minister Morris appointed a High Cost of Living Commission to investigate the allegations. It released a series of six reports, which confirmed suspicions that merchants were artificially inflating prices. For example, its report on flour, released in June 1917, revealed that dealers had hoarded supplies and charged unreasonably high prices. Merchants were making profits of $1.50 to $4 per barrel, instead of the pre-war profit of $0.50. They had made at least $600,000 in excess earnings, and the commissioners could find no reason to justify such large rate increases.

The reports added to the controversies that the government had to address. The commission's findings sparked calls for the conscription of wealth, while the collapse in recruiting sparked calls for the conscription of men. A growing dissatisfaction with the NPA pressured the government to play a larger role in administering the war effort.

All three political parties agreed that it was time to intervene. They formed a National Government in July 1917, which combined the People's Party, the Union Party, and the Liberals under a single coalition administration. The new executive consisted of six representatives from the People's Party and six from the combined Opposition (four Liberals and two Union Party members). The move restored some of the harmony of the early war

The *Bellaventure* was one of several steamers Newfoundland merchants sold to Russia during the war. *Archive (MHA), PF-055.2-H32*

years. Morris retired from politics at the end of the year, and Liberal leader William Lloyd replaced him as prime minister.

The new government worked quickly to address the problems that had plagued Newfoundland politics since 1916. In response to the public's discontent with merchants, it introduced a business profits tax in 1917, an income tax in 1918, and a wartime Ministry of Shipping and a Food Control Board.

It also created a Department of Militia to replace the NPA and direct the war effort. And it passed the Military Service Act on May 11, 1918, which brought conscription into effect—although the war ended before any of the conscripted troops saw active service. The national government remained in power for the duration of hostilities.

THE EVENING TELEGRAM, ST. JOHN'S, NEWFOUNDLAND

Foreigner Arrested!

SUSPECTED TO BE A GERMAN.

A foreigner who claims he is a Norwegian was arrested on suspicion last evening by Detectives Byrne and Lawlor. When brought to the police station he gave his name as Kristian Holti, while, according to the police, his name three months ago was Kristian Olsen. This foreigner was a seaman on board the schr. B. C. French, which is now overdue at Boston from here, and on board of which he injured a shipmate in October last and was arrested and convicted. He never went on board his vessel afterwards and has been going around the city every since, but shadowed by the police. A few days ago he attempted to sign on a local vessel but none of our seamen would sail with him as they believed he was a German. The police authorities had been making enquiries in the meantime and last night took him into custody. He will be kept in custody until he is able to give a satisfactory account of himself.

Fear and Loathing in Newfoundland

They called it "spy fever": an irrational fear that all German, Austro-Hungarian, and Turkish immigrants living in Allied countries, as well as their descendants, would forsake their adopted homes in a heartbeat and thwart the Allied war effort. It started in the United Kingdom, but it soon reached Newfoundland.

About 121 "enemy aliens" were living on the island when the war began. In December 1914, Newfoundland's governor Sir Walter Davidson described them as "harmless" in a letter to Lewis Harcourt, the Secretary of State for the Colonies. But that opinion was not shared by the wider public, nor by the press.

"Foreigner Arrested! Suspected to Be a German," the *Evening Telegram* headlined on January 6, 1915. It reported that, a few days earlier, the prisoner had "attempted to sign on a local vessel but none of our seamen would sail with him as they believed he was a German … He will be kept in custody until he is able to give a satisfactory account of himself."

By the time the war ended, Newfoundland had interred or deported about 60 "alien enemies." Among them was the American artist Rockwell Kent, who had moved to Brigus in 1914. After Kent publicly uttered pro-German sentiments, the Newfoundland government had him deported in July 1915. Newfoundland premier Joseph Smallwood officially apologized to Kent in 1968: "It is a dark guilt we have been carrying, sir, and you have been generous enough, kind enough, to allow us to wipe it off our soul, off our conscience."

37

World War I had lasted far longer than anyone had anticipated. By 1918, the extreme trauma of trench warfare was taking a heavy toll on many of the soldiers; this was reflected in their letters home.

"The war still rolls on and one almost begins to wonder how such a thing as war really is could possibly last longer than a week at the most, and how the people engaged in it can last for a day of real hard fighting," Lieutenant Henry Mews wrote to his Aunt Nell on March 22, 1918. "The war of the olden days was at least a fair and square fight, but in these days unseen people plank shells, etc. down ... consequently both sides just wait and trust to luck."

Thomas Ricketts

Thomas Ricketts was born at Middle Arm, White Bay, on April 15, 1901. His attestation papers report that he was 18 years and three months old when he joined the Newfoundland Regiment on September 2, 1916, but he was, in fact, only 15. After completing his training in St. John's, Ricketts departed for Europe on January 30, 1917, and was sent to France in June. A gunshot wound in the leg sent him to hospital in November 1917, but he returned to action in April 1918 and served with the Regiment for the remainder of the war. On January 19, 1919, King George V presented Ricketts with the Victoria Cross for his actions at Ledegem, Belgium. Ricketts also received the Belgian Croix de Guerre and was promoted to the rank of sergeant. After the war, Ricketts returned to Newfoundland, where he graduated from Memorial University College and later opened his own pharmacy. He died on February 10, 1967.

Josiah Robert Goodyear with his mount and a group of unidentified soldiers, n.d.
The Rooms Provincial Archives Division, B-3-10

The Royal Newfoundland Regiment was once again on the battlefield in April 1918, as part of the Lys Offensive. It fought near the northern French town of Bailleul for 10 days, until French soldiers relieved them on April 21. The Regiment suffered 176 casualties at Bailleul—another heavy blow.

It would take months for recruiters in Newfoundland and Labrador to supply enough men to bring the Regiment back up to fighting strength, so Allied commanders decided to remove it from the front lines. For the next few months, the Regiment guarded Field Marshal Haig's headquarters in Montreuil.

Its temporary removal from active operations also meant that the Royal Newfoundland Regiment was no longer attached to the 29th Division, a unit it had served with for two and a half years. The Division's commander, Major General Douglas Cayley, praised the Regiment in his farewell message on April 24, 1918:

"In bidding goodbye to the Royal Newfoundland Regiment on their departure from the 29th Division, I wish to place on record my very great regret at their withdrawal from a Division in which they have served so long and so brilliantly. The whole of their active service since September, 1915, has been performed in this Division, and during all that time the Battalion has shown itself to be, under all circumstances of good and bad fortune, a splendid fighting unit. At Suvla, Beaumont-Hamel, Gueudecourt, Monchy, Ypres, Cambrai, and during the late fighting near Bailleul, they have consistently maintained the highest standard of fighting efficiency and determination. They can look back on a record of which they and their fellow-countrymen have every right to be proud."

The Regiment remained at Montreuil for the spring

The St. John's Daily Star
Newfoundland

| VOLUME V. | ($3.00 per Annum) | WEDNESDAY, JANUARY 8, 1919. | (PROBS : Strong S. E. Winds; Milder) | No. |

STORY OF HEROIC DEED FOR WHICH THE V. C. WAS AWARDED PTE. RICKETTS, OF NFLD. REGT

WILL TAKE *Lemburg Is*   London, Jan. 7.—(via Reuter's Ottawa Agency   MANIAN

Lieut. Henry Mews in France on rest from the front line, 1918. *ASC, Coll. 267 2.01.006*

and summer of 1918. In September, it once again had sufficient numbers to return to action: 724 soldiers and a full complement of officers. By then, the Allies had launched their Hundred Days Offensive—a series of attacks against enemy forces that would ultimately push the Germans from France and end the war.

On September 28, 1918, the Royal Newfoundland Regiment was again in the trenches on the Ypres front, this time attached to the 28th Infantry Brigade of the 9th (Scottish) Division. It became involved in a two-day offensive to seize control of German strongpoints and to push the Allied front deeper into enemy territory.

The Regiment captured all of its objectives and advanced its line by 14.5 kilometres, at a cost of 100 casualties. It retreated to the village of Keiberg for a brief period of rest before entering the trenches at Ledegem on October 2. It spent four days there and successfully defended the Allied front line from a German counterattack.

On October 14, the Regiment fought in the Battle of Courtrai, near the village of Ledegem in the Belgian province of West Flanders. Its assignment was to move toward the River Lys and secure a railway track running north of Courtrai. The mission almost failed when the Regiment suddenly ran out of ammunition while under heavy enemy fire, but Private Thomas Ricketts volunteered to double back and retrieve the supplies.

The 17-year-old had to run through enemy fire, but he managed to retrieve the desperately needed ammunition. His selfless act of heroism allowed the Regiment to capture important enemy territory and eight POWs. It also earned Ricketts the Victoria Cross, which is the highest award for valour a Commonwealth serviceman can receive.

In the coming days, the Regiment continued its advance into enemy territory. It crossed the River Lys on October 20 and then proceeded toward the village of Vichte. By then, the war was almost over and Germany had entered into armistice talks with the Allies. On October 26, the Royal Newfoundland Regiment was withdrawn from front-line service altogether. It had lost 93 soldiers since September 28.

Blue Puttee Leave

Periods of leave were short, rare, and enormously valuable to the men of the Newfoundland Regiment. But it was not always a priority. At the beginning of the war, there was no such thing as soldier's leave. As everyone expected the fighting to end in a few months, it seemed unthinkable to sacrifice fighters to vacation time. That changed in the winter of 1915, when the true scope of the war became apparent. Instead of signing on for a few months of service, soldiers found themselves engaged in a multi-year battle. Commanders recognized that boosting troop morale would be vital to victory, and granting periods of leave was one of the best ways to do that. A soldier's leave was typically short and infrequent—a week or two per year.

The limits of travel often made it impossible for troops to return to Newfoundland and Labrador, so many of the soldiers took advantage of the time off to tour Europe. They visited the pyramids or travelled in the United Kingdom, where local charities helped to lodge and entertain Allied troops. Some of them fell in love with local women and came home with European brides. The biggest morale boost of all came in the summer of 1918, when the Royal Newfoundland Regiment granted a special "Blue Puttee Leave" to its First Five Hundred recruits—eight weeks off. Most of the men took advantage of the opportunity to return home and reconnect with family and loved ones.

WARM WELCOME FOR OUR HEROES

St. John's Does Honor To Veterans —Great Reception

ST. JOHN'S did honor to some of the Dominion's heroes in a royal manner last evening. It was a genuine Newfoundland welcome home to the first batch of 'blue puttees' or the first five hundred that left St. John's to fight for King and Country.

Everyone, old and young, that could get out last evening were present to honor the boys.

Shortly after 6.30 the signal gun near Cabot Tower acquainted the city that the Kyle would arrive in half an hour, and thousands hurried to the Furness Withy pier where she was to land.

No event in many years brought out so many people as did the arrival of these lads last evening.

Gaily the Kyle steamed through the Narrows and soon after she lay snugly at the pier and the boys were home again. Home after nearly four years of war; no wonder they were delighted.

Great Excitement

The thousands of citizens were most excited.

"They're coming!" someone shouted and this increased the excitement. The first soldier appeared—Mike Smythe—the same as ever grinning all over his face. Everyone knew he would, and they were not astray. The crowd just cheered him madly.

Then the others appeared and were no less enthusiastically received. Slowly the heroes passed through lines of intensely excited humanity. Cheering, hand shaking and kissing were the order.

Many of the lads were broken in body, not a few badly, but not one was broken in spirit. All were as enthusiastic as the day they left, while one brought the tears to many eyes as he waved his crutch and cheered for Newfoundland.

There were one hundred and seventy-seven in the party including 15

39

DEMOBILIZING THE REGIMENT

The Regiment entered Germany on December 4 and crossed the Rhine nine days later. The atmosphere was much less friendly there, partly due to orders from Allied commanders forbidding their troops from fraternizing with the local Germans. The Regiment remained in Germany until mid-February, when it was transferred to Rouen, France, to guard German POWs.

Royal Newfoundland Regiment crossing the Rhine into Germany, December 13, 1918.
The Rooms Provincial Archives Division, VA-28-146

The end of the war was already in sight when the Royal Newfoundland Regiment left the front lines on October 26, 1918. The Central powers were fragmenting and Germany's military situation was hopeless. Turkey signed an armistice on October 30, followed by Austria-Hungary on November 3. Finally, Germany signed the Armistice of Compiègne on November 11, which ended the war.

The Newfoundland Regiment was in reserve positions at Cuerne, Belgium, when peace was restored. Although the fighting was over, the men had to remain overseas for a few more months. They were ordered to Germany to serve as part of the occupation force and their assignment was to occupy a series of bridgeheads on the River Rhine.

From November 14 until December 4, the soldiers marched through Belgium, which was newly liberated from German occupation and showing the scars of a terrible war. Roads and railways were ripped apart, buildings reduced to crumbling heaps, and fields blasted into rubble. Amid all the devastation, the Newfoundlanders and Labradorians were warmly received by the villagers, who greeted them with cheers and thanks.

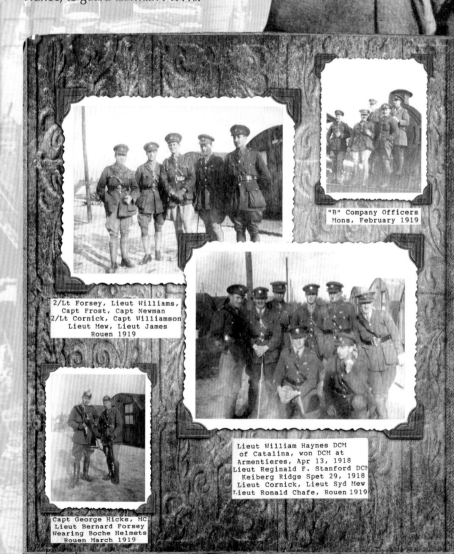

"B" Company Officers
Mons, February 1919

2/Lt Forsey, Lieut Williams, Capt Frost, Capt Newman 2/Lt Cornick, Capt Williamson Lieut Mew, Lieut James Rouen 1919

Lieut William Haynes DCM of Catalina, won DCM at Armentieres, Apr 13, 1918 Lieut Reginald F. Stanford DCM Keiberg Ridge Spet 29, 1918 Lieut Cornick, Lieut Syd Mew Lieut Ronald Chafe, Rouen 1919

Capt George Hicks, MC Lieut Bernard Forsey Wearing Boche Helmets Rouen March 1919

In April, the Regiment was transferred to England to enjoy shore leave and to prepare for the long-awaited voyage home. The largest draft of returning soldiers arrived at St. John's on June 1, 1919. It was pouring rain that day, but when the 956 men stepped off the RMS *Corsican*, a huge crowd welcomed them home. Some of them had not seen their families for years.

Lieut McHenry
Staff Sgt Hillier
Capt Williamson MC
CSM Fred Mercer
Rouen Apr 1919

"B" Company Cooker, en route to Rouen from Germany February 1919

Lieut Calder HAC
Capt Chafe MC
Lieut Stanford DCM
Lieut McHenry C de G
Rouen Mar 1919

Capt Hicks MC
Lieut McHenry C de G
Capt McNeil
Lieut R. Chafe
Capt Newman MC
Rouen Mar 1919

Food at the Front

After a long day of marching, digging trenches, or fighting, soldiers had little to look forward to in the way of culinary delights. Biscuits and bully-beef were trench staples. The biscuits were hard enough to crack a tooth on and the beef was tinned and salt-cured. Sound advice: pierce the tin before opening it—if it made a hissing sound, the meat was unfit for eating.

Jam, cheese, tea, and condensed milk were also common rations, but fresh bread was rare and fresh meat rarer still. Fruits and vegetables were so scarce that some men risked their lives to get them—they would run into No Man's Land to snatch a cabbage, potato, or raspberry growing there.

It was a little better in the reserve lines, where army cooks and mobile kitchens prepared meals. But the ingredient list was limited and cooks improvised with local ingredients, scrounging for wild mushrooms, nettles, and other edible plants. In the middle of war, it was difficult to get food to the field, so feeding the hundreds of thousands of soldiers anything at all was a stunning logistical achievement for Allied forces.

The situation improved when the men were billeted in living quarters away from the front lines. If they were in villages, the local people might give or sell them food, although the slowness of imports might also make this impossible. If the Regiment was billeted on a farm or large estate, the men were sometimes able to harvest their own food. Regiment officers were often inclined to turn a blind eye if their men seized the occasional chicken or poached local game. While billeting at a chateau in France, one innovative soldier even used his gas mask to harvest honey from one of the estate's hives.

It was a cause for celebration when anyone received a parcel in the mail and the men anxiously awaited gifts of chocolate, cakes, candy, sugar, canned meat, preserved berries, and other tastes of home.

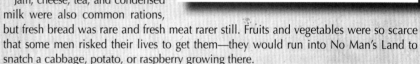

The Royal Newfoundland Regiment disbanded on August 26, 1919. What had begun as an ill-equipped and inexperienced group of civilians in 1914 had evolved into a respected unit of the British Army and the pride of the Newfoundland and Labrador people.

The Regiment had won 16 Battle Honours and 284 individual honours and awards. Of the 6,241 men who enlisted, 1,305 were killed, 2,314 wounded, and about 180 became POWs.

In subsequent years, many memorials were established to honour the Regiment, both at home and overseas. In Europe, five bronze caribou memorials were built on the battlegrounds where the Regiment had fought. A century later, they remain places of pilgrimage for people who want to honour the Royal Newfoundland Regiment. They go to remember its victories and to mourn the tragic sacrifices that too many of its fine men made in World War I.

PART THREE
OTHER FORCES

"We were under a very heavy fire, and we knew we couldn't hold on much longer. The boat was riddled and filling with water. We got rid of our packs and swam for the hopper, just in time, as a shell blew our boat to pieces."

—*H.T. Wells, Newfoundland Royal Naval Reserve*

"The sight and sound of his pain was so awful that once, when I went to the bathroom with a tray full of dressings, I found myself panting and had to lean against the wall. Then I remembered that every second of waiting meant pain for him."

—*Sybil Johnson, VAD*

Petty officers of the Newfoundland Royal Naval Reserve, n.d.
The Rooms Provincial Archives Division, F 46-25

HMS *Calypso* sailed into St. John's harbour on October 15, 1902. It carried a permanent complement of 28 instructors, all from the British Royal Navy, and could accommodate up to 300 volunteers. The Newfoundland Royal Naval Reserve accepted single men who were in good health, had seafaring experience, and were between the ages of 18 and 30. The upper age limit was dropped to 25 in 1909.

Most of the 375 men who volunteered in the first year were fishers from Newfoundland's Avalon Peninsula and northeast coast. They signed up for a five-year period and agreed to report to the *Calypso* once every year for 28 days of training. The government paid the expenses of outport reservists who had to travel to and from St. John's for training. The men could complete their training at a time of their choosing, and almost all of them arrived at St. John's during the winter months, when the fishing season was over and the seal hunt had not yet begun.

Calypso's commander Anthony Mac-Dermott was impressed by the quality of the recruits: "The Newfoundlanders took to naval life and routine like ducks to water," he later wrote in the first volume of the *Book of Newfoundland*. "These men, hitherto quite unaccustomed to discipline of any kind, never gave the smallest trouble to their officers. Their conduct was uniformly

Long before World War I broke out, Britain's Royal Navy recognized the skill and versatility of Newfoundland and Labrador seafarers, many of whom were outport fishers. The men, used to working in rough North Atlantic waters, could handle almost any kind of ship, from the small dories and punts that fished in inshore waters to the larger schooners and decked vessels that sailed to the Grand Banks and the Labrador coast. They were equally at home on the powerful steamers that braved the North Atlantic ice floes every spring to hunt seals.

In the fall of 1900 the British Admiralty invited 50 volunteers from Newfoundland and Labrador to complete a six-month training cruise aboard HMS *Charybdis*.

In 1902, the Newfoundland government and the British Admiralty recruited volunteers into a reserve force—a pool of well-trained sailors the Royal Navy could access in the event of war. The vessel left St. John's in November and sailed to the West Indies and back. Two more voyages over the next two years were so successful that the British and Newfoundland governments decided to station a permanent training ship at St. John's.

Newfoundland reservists training aboard HMS *Calypso* in St. John's, ca. 1916.
MHA, PF-319.227

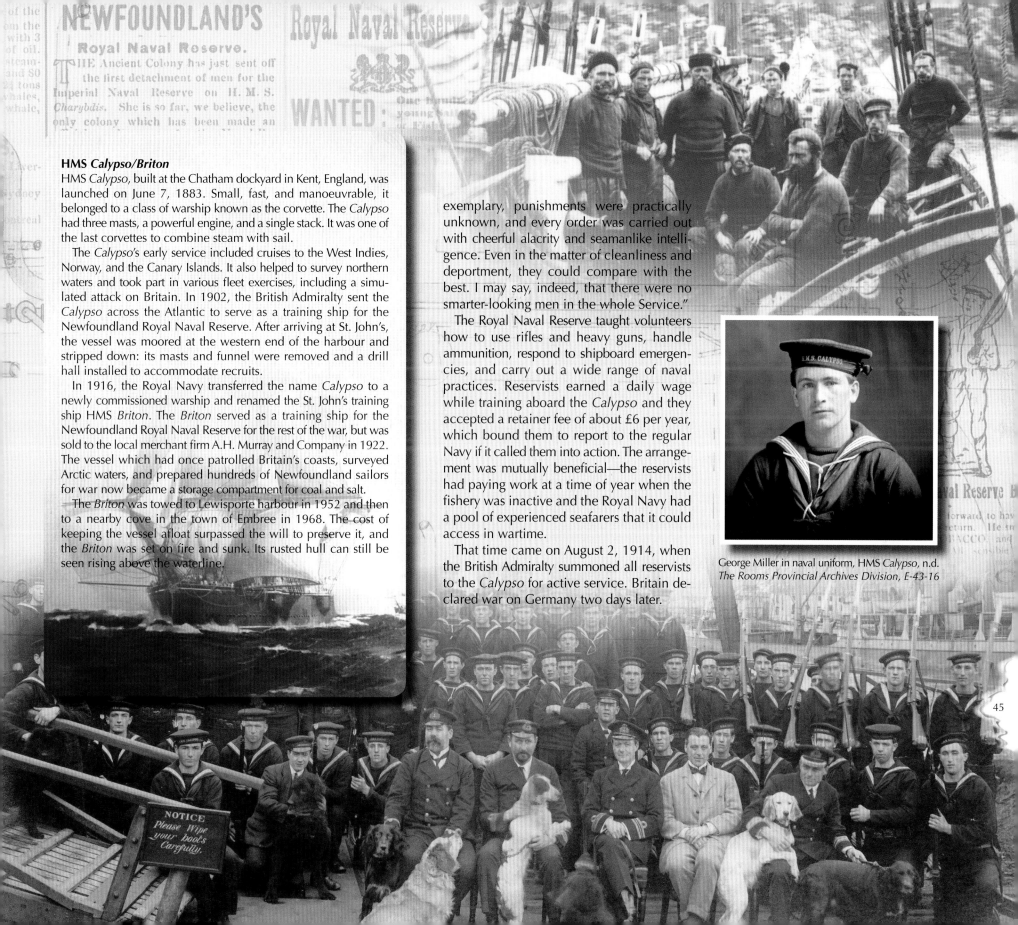

HMS *Calypso/Briton*

HMS *Calypso*, built at the Chatham dockyard in Kent, England, was launched on June 7, 1883. Small, fast, and manoeuvrable, it belonged to a class of warship known as the corvette. The *Calypso* had three masts, a powerful engine, and a single stack. It was one of the last corvettes to combine steam with sail.

The *Calypso*'s early service included cruises to the West Indies, Norway, and the Canary Islands. It also helped to survey northern waters and took part in various fleet exercises, including a simulated attack on Britain. In 1902, the British Admiralty sent the *Calypso* across the Atlantic to serve as a training ship for the Newfoundland Royal Naval Reserve. After arriving at St. John's, the vessel was moored at the western end of the harbour and stripped down: its masts and funnel were removed and a drill hall installed to accommodate recruits.

In 1916, the Royal Navy transferred the name *Calypso* to a newly commissioned warship and renamed the St. John's training ship HMS *Briton*. The *Briton* served as a training ship for the Newfoundland Royal Naval Reserve for the rest of the war, but was sold to the local merchant firm A.H. Murray and Company in 1922. The vessel which had once patrolled Britain's coasts, surveyed Arctic waters, and prepared hundreds of Newfoundland sailors for war now became a storage compartment for coal and salt.

The *Briton* was towed to Lewisporte harbour in 1952 and then to a nearby cove in the town of Embree in 1968. The cost of keeping the vessel afloat surpassed the will to preserve it, and the *Briton* was set on fire and sunk. Its rusted hull can still be seen rising above the waterline.

exemplary, punishments were practically unknown, and every order was carried out with cheerful alacrity and seamanlike intelligence. Even in the matter of cleanliness and deportment, they could compare with the best. I may say, indeed, that there were no smarter-looking men in the whole Service."

The Royal Naval Reserve taught volunteers how to use rifles and heavy guns, handle ammunition, respond to shipboard emergencies, and carry out a wide range of naval practices. Reservists earned a daily wage while training aboard the *Calypso* and they accepted a retainer fee of about £6 per year, which bound them to report to the regular Navy if it called them into action. The arrangement was mutually beneficial—the reservists had paying work at a time of year when the fishery was inactive and the Royal Navy had a pool of experienced seafarers that it could access in wartime.

That time came on August 2, 1914, when the British Admiralty summoned all reservists to the *Calypso* for active service. Britain declared war on Germany two days later.

George Miller in naval uniform, HMS *Calypso*, n.d.
The Rooms Provincial Archives Division, E-43-16

45

With Britain at war, the Royal Navy suddenly needed as many sailors as it could get, so the Newfoundland government suggested that it increase the size of the reserve to 1,000 men. London agreed. Enlistment requirements were broadened to encourage more men to sign up—reservists no longer had to have any previous seafaring experience and the maximum age limit was raised from 25 to 35. Approximately 660 volunteers came forward in the first six months, but about one-third of them were rejected on medical grounds.

Sailors were among the first people from Newfoundland and Labrador to see active service during the war. One month after hostilities broke out, 107 Newfoundland reservists were assigned to the Canadian Navy's HMCS *Niobe*. They searched the Strait of Belle Isle for German cruisers and spent 10 months patrolling the waters around New York and Boston. After the *Niobe*'s boilers failed in July 1915, the vessel was decommissioned and the Newfoundlanders sent to Britain for reassignment.

Gallipoli Landings: An Eyewitness Account

In the spring of 1915, some Newfoundland reservists were deployed to the Mediterranean, near the Gallipoli Peninsula. The Allied powers wanted to seize control of the peninsula from enemy forces, so they launched a series of naval and ground attacks. On April 25, they deployed thousands of soldiers to the area. They came by sea, and it was the Navy's job to ferry the men to the tip of the peninsula.

Newfoundland reservist H.T. Wells was one of the sailors who brought the soldiers to shore. As they approached land, they encountered a devastating barrage of enemy fire.

"By this time there were only two of us left at the oars, the remainder were lying in the bottom of the boat, either dead or wounded, some of them dressing the others wounds," Wells later wrote for *The Veteran* in 1936. "An officer on shore shouted to us to jump overboard and swim for it. Both of us jumped out and tried to swim to the hopper, but we found our packs too heavy, and returned to our boat. We hung on to the lifelines for a few minutes, as we could not get into her, she was so high out of water. While hanging on the lines my mate got hit, a bullet running under his shirt and across his shoulders, cutting into his shoulder-blade.

"We were under a very heavy fire, and we knew we couldn't hold on much longer. The boat was riddled and filling with water. We got rid of our packs and swam for the hopper, just in time, as a shell blew our boat to pieces. We reached the hopper in an exhausted condition, so we sat down under what we thought was cover. But we soon found that we were being sniped and my mate got one right through the breast and I was left alone, and joined up with another boat."

Newfoundland sailors in Europe, ca. 1914-19
MHA, PF-001.1-Q12a

World War I Q-boats.
MHA PF-000.1-Q06a, PF-ooo1.1-Q05a.

By then, the Newfoundland Royal Naval Reserve had reached its target of 1,000 men. New recruits were drilled on the *Calypso* in St. John's and then sent to England for further training.

Unlike the men of the Newfoundland Regiment, who remained with their unit, reservists were scattered throughout the Royal Navy. They served on mine-sweeping trawlers near the British Isles and on armed merchant vessels, travelling to such places as India, Africa, South America, and Australia. Newfoundlanders and Labradorians served as gunners and deckhands, landed ground troops in warzones, and shipped desperately needed food and equipment to Allied ports.

Newfoundland reservists also served on Q-boats: heavily armed naval vessels that were disguised to look like simple merchant ships or fishing boats. A Q-boat's job was to lure enemy submarines close enough to be fired upon. It took nerves of steel for the men to wait quietly while a U-boat prowled nearby.

Of the 16 Newfoundland reservists who are known to have served on Q-boats in foreign waters, only one died. Seaman John Joseph Power was killed on March 29, 1917, when his vessel collided with the SS *Tainu* off the Isle of Wight. He was 18 years old.

"Every man-jack of them"

Although 600 men were enrolled in the Newfoundland Royal Naval Reserve when hostilities broke out, Navy officials were concerned that not everyone would respond to the call to duty.

"This, it should be remembered, was during the height of the fishing season, and to be called away from their work at this time naturally entailed great hardship and serious financial loss to these poor fellows," Commander Anthony MacDermott wrote. "The fishing season in Newfoundland is of short duration and during it the fishermen have to earn enough to keep themselves and their families for the whole year. 'You'll never get them!' I was told. 'You can't expect men to give up their livelihood for a war they know nothing about, and in which they have no concern.'

"Well, being new to the country, I kept an open mind on the subject. But the croakers were wrong. I did get them—every man-jack of them—and with no trouble at all, though many of them had to walk fifty or sixty miles to the nearest steamer or railway station."

47

NEWFOUNDLAND RESERVISTS ON PATROL

Some Newfoundland reservists who went overseas served with the Royal Navy's 10th Cruiser Squadron. This unit formed at the start of the war to patrol the North Sea and the waters between the British Isles and Iceland. Its goals were to cut Germany off from overseas trade and to prevent its warships from entering the Atlantic Ocean.

It was a dangerous patrol, marked by rough waters, heavy fog, and frequent gales. Enemy mines and torpedoes were other threats. The squadron suffered heavy losses. In mid-January 1915, HMS *Viknor* sank near Scotland's northwest coast. Everyone was killed, including 25 Newfoundlanders. There were no eyewitness accounts of the loss, but the vessel had been operating in bad weather and in an area recently mined by German warships.

About three weeks later, the armed merchant cruiser *Clan McNaughton* sank while patrolling the waters off Ireland's north coast. It was widely believed to have gone down in a heavy gale that struck the area on February 3. Among the dead were 22 Newfoundland reservists.

Reservists Philip Caines, Bob Bonnell, Peter Quirck, and Ernest Hillier, n.d.
Courtesy of Darrell Hillier

Eleven more reservists died on March 11, 1915, after a German U-boat torpedoed and sank HMS *Bayano*. The attack happened at 5:15 a.m. Among the 26 survivors was one from Newfoundland—Seaman Stephen Keates of Fogo. He continued to serve in the Navy until the end of the war.

Several of the Newfoundlanders who served in the 10th Cruiser Squadron were awarded for their skill and courage. Among them were Leander Greene, Albert Gregory, and Martin Pottle, who each received the Distinguished Service Medal for acts of bravery.

In addition to their service overseas, members of the Newfoundland Royal Naval Reserve also served at home. They formed a protective guard at the British Admiralty's wireless station in Mount Pearl and served at Fort Waldegrave, a battery overlooking the St. John's harbour. Reservists helped to build a barracks at the fort and the *Calypso* provided it with a 6-inch naval gun. Members of the local Legion of Frontiersmen manned the fort, but naval reservists assisted as gunners.

In 1915, Commander MacDermott created a Newfoundland and Labrador patrol to safeguard inshore waters and the Grand Banks fishery. Local coastal boats, such as the *Kyle*, *Prospero*, and *Fogota*, were armed with guns from the *Calypso* and manned by Newfoundland reservists. They patrolled local waters, keeping an eye out for U-boats and other

Grief Turned to Joy.

Yesterday the home of Mrs. Wheeler, Torbay Road, which has been the scene of mourning and sorrow since the loss of the Clan MacNaughton, was suddenly changed into one of joy. Mrs. Wheeler had been mourning the loss of her son Philip, who was believed to have been on the missing ship, when a letter from her boy came yesterday announcing the joyful news that he was quite safe. The following is his letter:

F. WARD,
Fizakerley Hospital, Liverpool,
February 26th.

My Dearest Mother,—Just a few lines hoping you are keeping quite well, as it leaves me at present. Dear mother, I am just writing to let you know I came off the Clan McNaughton before she went down, and I am quite safe. I am in this hospital with pneumonia, but I am glad to tell you I have got over the worst of it and I am progressing favorably, and hope to be out soon. So I have no more to say at present. Hoping to hear from you soon, I remain,

Your loving son,
PHILIP.

P.S.—Please mother remember me to all at home.

Another letter was received from Sister Ryder, of the Hospital, who writes as follows:

WARD F.,
1st Western General Hospital,
Fizakerley, March 1st, 1915.

Dear Mrs. Wheeler,—I do not know if your son Philip has written to you since he has been in this Hospital, but seeing his name amongst the names of those brave men missing from H.M.S. Clan MacNaughton, I thought perhaps you would be relieved to hear he has been in this hospital since the 20th of January. He has been very ill with typhoid fever, but is now doing very well, and we hope that he will soon be up and about again.

Yours sincerely,
(Sister) H. RYDER.

The gladness which these rays of heavenly sunshine brought to that humble dwelling on the Torbay Road yesterday, can better be imagined than described. The story of Philip Wheeler's escape is a remarkable one....

Evening Telegram, March 23, 1915.

The Order of the White Feather

As the number of war dead climbed, so too did the armed forces' need for volunteers. By 1916, recruiting propaganda that had initially appealed to the public's patriotism and sense of duty also tried to shame men into volunteering. War posters adopted slogans like "Get into Khaki—We Are Doing OUR Bit" or "Your Chums Are Fighting—Why Aren't YOU?"

Local newspaper editorials also tried to pressure men into enlisting: "Young men of Newfoundland, the need for your services grows more insistent with the passing weeks. Which part will you choose—Soldier, or Slacker?" the *St. John's Daily Star* asked on February 2, 1916.

By then, the Order of the White Feather had arrived in Newfoundland. It was founded at the start of the war by Admiral Charles Fitzgerald of the Royal Navy and eventually spread throughout the British Empire. The Order's campaign asked women to give white feathers—a symbol of cowardice—to men of military age who had not yet enlisted. It became such a problem in Newfoundland that even some local newspapers, which were usually quick to support the war effort, called for restraint. The following appeared in the *St. John's Daily Star* on April 14, 1917:

"In more than one instance, young fellows have undeservedly been branded as cowards, who were probably just as brave and patriotic as many of their chums who volunteered, but, for private reasons were unable to go themselves. The inclination may have been there, but for certain circumstances they were unable to offer their services. These reasons may have been owing to some physical infirmity which the lad knew rendered him ineligible, but which from sensitiveness he did not care to confide about to others.

"There might too, have been family or financial reasons why it was necessary that he should remain at home, even though he might be physically fit.... I believe most of these feathers are sent thoughtlessly by young girls, who, not knowing all the circumstances, imagined they were doing something patriotic, when, as a matter of fact, they were mistaken in their judgement."

Young men also faced significant economic pressure to enlist. By 1917, merchant firms refused to accept any sealer under the age of 30 who had not applied for military service. This was particularly damaging to outport fishers and their families, who relied on the spring seal hunt to supplement their meagre earnings from the cod fishery.

The situation became so tense by the fall of 1916 that the dominion began issuing special badges to volunteers who had tried to enlist but were rejected for medical or other reasons. The badges were made of bronze and inscribed with the words "For King and Country I have offered."

signs of enemy activity. Although the force never did engage the enemy, it grew in importance as the U-boat menace spread to the western North Atlantic in the later stages of hostilities.

Between 1914 and 1918, about 2,000 men joined the Newfoundland Royal Naval Reserve, and about 200 died. The reserve disbanded in 1921.

"At the close of the war, every man of the Reserve had completed his agreed period of service, and took his discharge, so the famous Corps was automatically disbanded and ceased to exist," MacDermott wrote. "The *Calypso* (now called *Briton*) remained in commission for some time, and it was at first hoped that recruiting might be reopened and the Reserve revived; but the money was not forthcoming, so the old ship was paid off and sold, and 'finis' had to be written to a not inglorious chapter in Newfoundland history."

Silas Pittman of Woody Point. Sailor on HMS *Briton*, in uniform and kit. *MHA, PF-001.1-Q09a*

The St. John's Daily Star
Newfoundland

VOLUME II. ($3.00 per Annum.)   MONDAY, OCTOBER 9, 1916.   (Price: One Cent.)   No. 235.

STEPHANO WITH, FIVE OTHER STEAMERS, TORPEDOED BY U-53 OFF NANTUCKET, U.S.
All The Passengers And Crews Are Rescued

Two kinds of vessels were vital to the war at sea: fighting and freighting ships. The former were the battleships, destroyers, and various military vessels that belonged to the Royal Navy and other Allied forces; the latter were the tramps, trawlers, and other civilian ships of the Merchant Navy which transported people, food, munitions, and other goods to Allied ports.

Without the merchant fleet, the Allied war effort would likely have ended in failure. Britain was the nerve centre of the Allied powers, but it depended heavily on imports. During the war, German U-boats tried to disrupt the trade routes that linked Britain to North America and the rest of the world—the goal was to weaken the Empire by depriving its people and army of food and supplies.

As a result, manning a merchant vessel became dangerous work and civilian crew members faced constant threat of U-boat attack. If their vessel was sunk, they risked death or becoming POWs. The most dangerous waters included the North Atlantic, the Mediterranean, the White Sea, and all waters surrounding France and the United Kingdom.

On October 20, 1914, the German U-boat U-17 sank the British steamship *Giltra* while it was carrying coal, oil, and other goods to Stavanger, Norway. The *Giltra* was the first British merchant vessel destroyed in the war. By the time the fighting ended four years later, more than 3,000 British merchant vessels had been lost and nearly 15,000 seafarers killed; another 3,200 became POWs.

More than 500 Newfoundlanders and Labradorians are known to have served in the Merchant Navy. The dominion's overwhelming dependence on maritime trade and its deeply rooted seafaring traditions meant that its sailors often worked in dangerous waters. They fished in the North Atlantic, they shipped goods to and from Britain, the Mediterranean, Brazil, and the Carribbean, and they plied the passenger trade along North America's east coast. They were also dispersed, in ones, twos, and threes, on hundreds of British merchant vessels operating across the globe.

At the start of hostilities, Newfoundland's waters were relatively safe, but as the war progressed, German U-boats became increasingly common in the western Atlantic. On October 8, 1916, one of them torpedoed and sank the SS *Stephano* off the coast of Massachusetts. The *Stephano*, a Newfoundland steamer, had been carrying passengers from St. John's to New York. No one died in the attack and American destroyers rescued everyone on board.

Another U-boat captured a Canadian trawler on the Grand Banks on August

---

The Royal Navy's Rear-Admiral John Ernest Troyte Harper on the Importance of the Merchant Navy

"In time of war the combatant which can ensure the safe passage of its own merchant ships and transports, while denying the same to the enemy, may be said to have attained 'command of the sea.'

"How then did the sea power of our Empire come into being? It came through our merchant ships; those ships of all descriptions which have ploughed the seas, under sail or steam, in fair weather or foul, under that flag which every seaman respects—the Red Ensign, or its predecessor." (*The Veteran* 8.1 [1929])

20, 1918, and several other boats were attacked or seized in the vicinity over the next 10 days. Among them was a Newfoundland steamer, the *Erik*, which sank on August 25. One of its passengers was Lance Corporal John Ryan of the Royal Newfoundland Regiment. He survived the attack and his account appeared in the

The SS Erik. MHA, PF-315.197; Evening Telegram, September 2, 1918.

Evening Telegram on September 2, 1918:

"I went around to see where all the men were, when the cabin windows came in with a click and the lamp was blown out. A shell had burst on the derrick and wounded the mate who was on the bridge; the same shell cut the derrick and it dropped to the deck, it also carried away a lot of the rigging and part of the wireless aerial. I left the cabin and went forward to the forecastle, and then several shells hit the ship in quick succession around the engine room. The boiler was letting off steam like a huge kettle, and shoots of flame made their appearance around the smoke stack. We thought the ship was on fire but the flames died down when the firing ceased. The deck was honeycombed by shell fire and it was dangerous to move around. Nobody saw the sub until she hove up alongside over half an hour later."

The *Erik* was lost, but the Germans saved all the crew and passengers and brought them to a Newfoundland schooner that was fishing in the area.

Not all mercantile marines were that lucky. On April 3, 1918, the U-boat U-152 torpedoed and sank the Newfoundland schooner *Elsie Burdette* while it was carrying a cargo of salt from Oporto, Portugal, to Newfoundland. All six crew members were from Newfoundland and all were lost at sea. Their names are inscribed on a memorial at Beaumont-Hamel: Ward Strickland, John Hatcher, Albert Hann, John Evans, Henry Dicks, and Ward Collier.

Sometimes the Germans took the sailors as prisoners. On June 18, 1918, a U-boat captured the Newfoundland schooner *Dictator* while it was transporting a cargo of salt from Cadiz, Spain, to Newfoundland. The *Dictator*'s six crew members became POWs and were sent to Germany. Two of them, Leo Bungay and James Parsons, died in captivity. The other four, Thomas Fireman, Edgar Banfield, Charles Blydon, and Thomas Bowridge, returned to Newfoundland in January 1919.

At least 115 merchant mariners from Newfoundland and Labrador are known to have died in World War I. Their names are inscribed on memorials at Beaumont-Hamel in France and at Bowring Park in St. John's.

Defensive Measures

Allied forces employed various strategies to protect their merchant vessels. One method was known as "dazzle camouflage." Ships were painted in bold patterns and sharply contrasting colours that made them look like giant tigers and jaguars stalking the ocean's surface. Rather than conceal the vessel, the patterns were intended to confuse the enemy. When viewed through a submarine's periscope, the jagged lines, curves, and other patterns distorted the vessel's form to make it look as though it was facing the opposite direction or travelling at a different speed than it actually was.

A second defensive strategy was the armed convoy system. Beginning in 1917, some merchant vessels travelled in large groups under the escort of warships. This innovation meant that German U-boats had to search a larger area for fewer targets. Some merchant vessels were also outfitted with guns and manned by Royal Naval Reservists.

51

NEWFOUNDLAND FORESTRY CORPS

The Newfoundland Forestry Corps was a non-combatant military unit that was formed in April 1917 to supply Britain with the lumber it needed for the war effort. Instead of fighting on the front lines, the Forestry Corps's loggers and sawmill workers served in the United Kingdom's forests.

Britain's demand for timber skyrocketed during the war. Its armed forces needed wood to build dugout shelters, to line muddy trench floors, and to provide stakes for the thousands of kilometres of barbed wire that stretched across the front lines. New railroads had to be built to transport soldiers and equipment across the Western Front, and the munitions industry depended on a steady supply of wood to serve as frames in its mines so that it could gather the huge quantities of iron ore it needed to manufacture weapons and ammunition.

But just as Britain's need for timber increased, its supply was almost cut off. The UK imported much of its lumber from Canada; during the war, German U-boats disrupted the maritime trade routes that linked North America with Europe. Soon, Britain was forced to set aside much of its already depleted cargo space for more critical imports such as food and ammunition.

By 1916, the British government was facing a crisis. As Britain could not import enough lumber to meet its needs, it decided to harvest local forests. The only problem: insufficient loggers and sawmill workers in the UK. Britain asked Canada if it could provide a battalion of lumbermen.

The response was enthusiastic: within six weeks of the request, 1,600 men volunteered. The first 400 arrived at England on April 12 and more followed in the coming years.

Newfoundland also offered to help. While Newfoundland prime minister Sir Edward Morris was on a state visit to England in March 1917, he suggested that the dominion create a 500-man Forestry Corps. The British government offered to pay the costs of raising and maintaining the unit, while the NPA assumed the responsibility for recruiting men.

Newfoundland governor Sir Walter Davidson issued a call for recruits on April 4, 1917. Enlistment requirements were more relaxed than those for the armed forces because the Forestry Corps was a non-combatant unit. Recruiters accepted able-bodied men of any age and height, and Davidson wrote that "no one shall be rejected for eyesight, flat feet, loss of fingers, deafness, etc." However, the Forestry Corps did not want to interfere with the military's recruiting efforts, so it rejected all single men who were eligible to join the Regiment or Naval Reserve.

Workers at a Newfoundland logging camp.
MHA, PF-107.001

Paper Towns Go to War

There was no shortage of experienced loggers in Newfoundland during the war. Commercial use of the dominion's forests had started in the second half of the 1800s, when the government made woodlots available to sawmill operators and paper companies. As the companies established mills in central and western Newfoundland, they also helped build new "paper towns" to accommodate workers. Grand Falls came into being almost overnight when the Anglo-Newfoundland Development Company opened a pulp and paper mill there in 1909. A rapid influx of settlers also arrived at Bishop's Falls after Albert E. Reed and Company established a pulp mill there in 1911. The general managers of both the Grand Falls and Bishop's Falls mills encouraged their staff to join the Forestry Corps and guaranteed that their jobs would be waiting for them after the war. As a result, one of the largest concentrations of volunteers to the Forestry Corps came from the Twillingate Electoral District, which included the paper towns of Grand Falls and Bishop's Falls.

In the end, about 500 volunteers joined the Newfoundland Forestry Corps. Another 278 were rejected on medical grounds. The first 99 recruits to the Newfoundland Forestry Corps departed St. John's aboard the SS *Florizel* on May 19, 1917, and more drafts followed at irregular intervals.

Recruits came from a wide demographic, including teenagers who were too young to join the armed forces and men who were too old to fight overseas. A few had served overseas, but were wounded so badly that they were sent home. That was the case with Lieutenant Hector Ross of the Newfoundland Regiment, who had been hit by an enemy shell at Gallipoli on November 4, 1915. His wounds put him in hospital for six months and removed him from active service altogether. When the Forestry Corps formed in 1917, he signed up and became its Adjutant Captain.

Hector Ross.
The Rooms Provincial Archives Division, VA 36-13

The Forestry Corps also accepted men of military age who had tried to join the Regiment or the Navy, but were rejected on medical grounds. Harry Willar of St. John's had applied to the army on three separate occasions, but was rejected each time as physically unfit.

Members of the Newfoundland Forestry Corps in Scotland, ca. 1917.
Courtesy of the Heritage Society of Grand Falls-Windsor

He wanted to go overseas so badly that he gave up a good paying job at the post office to join the Forestry Corps in 1917. Before he departed, he wrote the Colonial Secretary to suggest that volunteers should not lose their jobs because of their military service:

"I sent the post master general my resignation a few days ago, which takes effect November 30th to enable me to take up duty with the regiment December 1st. I felt it my duty to do something in the interest of my Country and therefore gave up a good situation, which I hope to get back again when I return. I am a married man and cannot afford to be idle when I come back. I trust the appointment to the position I am leaving will be only temporary as I am very anxious to have the assurance that my job will be OK again."

As a result of that letter, the Postmaster General promised Willar that when he returned from the war, he would have a job that was as good, or better, than the one he had left behind.

Once the Newfoundland foresters arrived overseas, they were ordered to the hillside forest of Craigvinean, located on the Duke of Atholl's estate at Dunkeld in central Scotland. Armed with axes and saws, the men worked from sunrise until sunset in the woods, first cutting a notch in the trunk with an axe, then felling the tree with a saw.

Moving the logs down the steep and difficult terrain to the mill site presented an early challenge. Local woodsmen believed a mountain railway would have to be built, but such a task would require significant time, resources, and money. Instead, the Newfoundlanders built a 900-metre-long chute that stretched from the top of the hill to a pond at the bottom, where the logs could be floated to the sawmill. The log chute was believed to have been the longest in the world at the time.

By early 1918, the Newfoundlanders had cleared 1,200 acres of timberland in Craigvinean and were transferred to the Scottish village of Kenmore, which lay about 40 kilometres to the east. They set up camp in an 800-acre forest that covered Drummond Hill and continued logging the area until hostilities ended. The Newfoundland Forestry Corps closed down its operations and sent its volunteers home in early 1919.

Today, a statue of a Newfoundland forester is part of the National War Memorial in downtown St. John's.

53

APPEAL FOR MEN

By His Excellency the Governor.

War can be won this year if every man comes forward.

Newfoundland Forestry Battalion to be raised.

AVIATORS

At least 21 people from Newfoundland and Labrador served as aviators during the war. They joined Britain's Royal Flying Corps (RFC), which merged with the Royal Naval Air Service in April 1918 to form the Royal Air Force (RAF).

Aviation was still in its pioneering stage when war broke out. The powered airplane was barely a decade old and aviators were still trying to complete the world's first non-stop transatlantic flight. By 1914, airplanes were dangerous, with crude, experimental designs. It was rumoured that RFC recruits had a better chance of being killed in training than in combat.

At the start of the war, aviators flew wooden and canvas biplanes that were highly flammable and could barely reach speeds of 100 miles per hour. Pilots carried service pistols to shoot at the enemy, but not parachutes, which were too bulky to cram into the cockpit and deemed unnecessary by military commanders who feared aviators would jump out at the first sign of danger.

The military, initially unsure of how to use airplanes, first used them for reconnaissance missions. Pilots were ordered to locate the enemy, observe their movements, and photograph trenches. As the war progressed, air combat grew in importance and the military's need for increasingly sophisticated warplanes pushed aviation technology to new frontiers.

Two new kinds of aircraft soon emerged—the fighter and the bomber. Fighters were small and agile and outfitted with machine guns, which meant that pilots no longer had to fire pistols at one another or throw grenades. Bombers were larger and less manoeuvrable and designed to deliver a heavy payload of explosives to a single target.

Aviators who flew these new aircraft took tremendous risks. The typical life expectancy for a combat pilot was just several weeks during the war, and that dropped to 21 days of active service in the spring of 1917. The high casualty rates meant that the RCF was in constant need of aviators, and it pushed new recruits through a few weeks of intensive training before thrusting them into active service. Most fighter pilots had no more than 15 hours of solo flying time when they reached an active front.

One of those pilots was Lieutenant Leonard Edens of St. John's. He received his flying certificate from the RFC on March 31, 1917, and was

John Henry Stanley Green (1890–1917)

John Henry Stanley Green was born in St. John's on July 20, 1890. When war broke out, he gave up his accounting job to become one of the Newfoundland Regiment's First Five Hundred recruits. He enlisted on September 2, 1914, and was given regimental number 108. Green travelled to Europe aboard the *Florizel* with the rest of the Blue Puttees. He trained at Salisbury Plains, England, and then went to Scotland to train at Fort George and Stobs Camp.

Green fought at Gallipoli in September 1915 but was removed from the front lines for medical reasons on October 3, 1915. He was diagnosed with pyrexia (fever) and taken to the 15th General Hospital in Alexandra, Egypt. His health prevented him from returning to the trenches for some time. He was stationed in the United Kingdom, where he likely performed administrative work at Regimental Headquarters.

On March 12, 1917, Green transferred to the RFC and became a flying officer with the 57th Squadron. In April 1917, he took part in the Battle of Arras as an observer. His job was to accompany the pilot, photograph the battleground, and assess enemy movements.

On July 7, 1917, Green was killed while taxiing his plane across uneven ground behind British lines. His propeller struck the ground and broke off, and the aircraft burst into flames. Green died instantly from extensive burns. He was buried at Longuenesse St. Omer Souvenir Cemetery in France. Green died two weeks before his 27th birthday.

Nfld. Airman

Lieut. Edens, R.F.C., Tells of His First Fighting in the Air.

The following interesting extracts are from letters received by Mr. T. J. Edens, from his son Leonard, of the Royal Flying Corps.

40th Squadron R. F. C.,
B. E. F. France,
Aug. 17th, '17.

Dear Mother and Dad:—

You of course know by this time that I am in France or if not it is not my fault, as I have sent two letters and a cable telling you, so that ought to be enough. I am now in the line but cannot, of course, say just where. I am very lucky in getting in this Squadron which is one of the best in France, they have an awfully fine bunch of fellows, and it is quite a comfy spot when not on duty. I have not yet been over the lines but have been quite close up to them. I hoped to see Mr. Rioux but was not able to, however I may manage it some time yet. At first I was very sorry to leave my own Squadron but I think I have a better chance by coming to a Squadron which is part of the line than if I came out with a new Squadron.

August 20th, 1917.

I told you in my last letter that I would probably have more to tell you than in the last; well, not so much as I thought, things have been wonderfully quiet for us. We have been in the air a lot looking for Huns but it has been a vain quest. I feel sure, however, that after to-morrow I will have more to tell; to-morrow is a big day for us and I start bright and early, there is to be another push in our part of the line and we have some very dangerous work to do; however, I feel sure that your prayers and my own will pull me through; any way I am quite prepared for whatever God's will may be and I hope and trust that He may see fit to spare me.

transferred to France. Edens described his first air fight in a letter home, which the *Evening Telegram* published on September 15, 1917:

"It is two days now since I had my baptism of fire and I tell you it's all it's cracked up to be and more. You go sailing securely through the air then there's a woof! woof! right under your tail, then you proceed to make yourself scarce. That is your introduction to the anti-aircraft gun, or 'Archie' as we call him. He is no friend of ours at all. Last night I had my first fight. We were on patrol well over the lines when we saw a crowd of Huns and attacked them. It was some show, about twenty machines all mixed up and firing their guns. It lasted about twenty minutes and then we went home as the Huns all buzzed off. The result was sort of indecisive. We saw three Huns go down but do not know whether they were done in. One of our fellows is missing."

Edens also went missing in an air fight over Roulers, Belgium, on March 18, 1918. Officials later learned that he died in enemy hands. He was 27 years old.

Edens was one of two Newfoundland airmen killed in the war. The other, John Henry Stanley Green of St. John's, began his military service in 1914 as one of the Newfoundland Regiment's First Five Hundred recruits. He fought at Gallipoli, but was removed from the front lines in October 1915 due to illness. He transferred to the RFC in March 1917, but his service was brief. On July 7, 1917, Green died from severe burns he sustained in a flying accident near St. Omer, France. His death notice appeared in local newspapers the following week.

Newfoundland Airplanes

Newfoundland did not just contribute pilots to the RFC—it also provided some of the planes. In 1915, the NPA solicited donations to its Aeroplane Fund and by the end of the year had raised enough money to put four Gnome Vickers biplanes in the sky. The Reid Newfoundland Company donated a fifth plane to the RCF. These aircraft were designated "Newfoundland Nos. 1 to 4" and "Reid Newfoundland."

As if to offset the sorrow of the daily casualty lists, local newspapers ran glowing profiles of the dominion's servicemen and servicewomen. In October 1917, a 19-year-old aviator named Ronald Ayre stole the headlines. He had won the Military Cross and a promotion to the rank of captain for conducting a series of successful bombing raids against the enemy.

"He is the first from the Island to attain so high rank in the flying service and, if we mistake not, to win a distinction," the *Evening Telegram* editorialized on October 10, 1917. "The list of Newfoundland aviators slowly grows larger and the same intrepidity that distinguishes the Regiment begins to make them out also in an arm of the forces where bravery is a byeword."

The *Daily Star* also praised Ayre: "Young Ayre was at school when he volunteered and he at once offered for aviation work. He was accepted, and having passed the examination brilliantly, he was sent to the front, and has since made heaps of trouble for the enemy."

One year later, a second aviator from Newfoundland was decorated for bravery in combat. Captain Victor Bennett of the RAF won the Croix de Guerre for his role in a bombing attack against German forces in France. A description of his actions can be found in his attestation papers:

"In commanding his platoon he has given proof of great courage and activity. On the 18th of July whilst carrying out a raiding expedition he conducted his patrol safely within the German lines where he encountered a squadron of 15 Aeroplanes which he succeeded in forcing to retreat, thus permitting his gunners to accomplish their mission. In a personal encounter he forced two of the enemies' machines to descend."

One of the dominion's aviators became a POW. John (Jack) Blackall was captured on May 21, 1917, after German fighter planes shot down his aircraft. Blackall remained a prisoner for the rest of hostilities and returned home safely after peace was restored.

Women from Newfoundland and Labrador were not allowed to enlist in the armed forces during World War I, but they could serve overseas with the Voluntary Aid Detachment (VAD). A unit of semi-trained nurses, the VADs performed a wide range of medical services.

The British Red Cross Society had formed the VAD in 1909 to provide auxiliary medical service in the event of war. During World War I, the VADs worked as hospital cooks, clerks, and maids; they assisted at operations; they cared for patients; and they drove ambulances. Basically, they did what they could to lessen the workload of the professional nurses with whom they served. As the war continued, hospitals became flooded

A group of VADs in England, n.d. *ASC, Coll. 158 8.10*

with badly wounded soldiers from the front lines and the VADs were thrust into work better suited to professional nurses.

Professional Nurses

Some Newfoundland and Labrador women served overseas as professional nurses. Among them was Maisie Parsons, who served in military hospitals at Belgium, Egypt, and Greece. Originally from the fishing community of Harbour Grace on Newfoundland's Avalon Peninsula, Parsons had graduated from the General Hospital's School of Nursing in St. John's. After war broke out, she joined the Canadian Army Medical Corps.

Frances Cron was another School of Nursing graduate who served overseas. She worked aboard the hospital ship *Carrisbrooke Castle*, which criss-crossed the English Channel, picking up wounded soldiers from French ports and bringing them back to England for treatment. It was dangerous work—German U-boats prowled the Channel and torpedoed Allied vessels. Mines were another threat. About 20 hospital ships sank during the war.

Frances Cron, second from right.

The VADs had to complete several weeks of training in St. John's before going overseas. They took courses in first aid, home nursing, and hygiene; they volunteered in local hospitals; and open-air drills taught them how to pitch hospital tents, care for wounded soldiers, and build and cook on campfires.

Frances Cluett of Belleoram, Fortune Bay, joined the VAD in 1916 and trained in St. John's. She described her experiences in the many letters she sent to her family.

"At 8 pm Mrs. Browning took me down to British Hall to the lecture room," she wrote home in mid-October (the exact date is not written on the letter). "I was just a little late. There were seven girls already there. Dr. Reeves lectured to us, then we had to apply bandages ourselves. I got an introduction to a Miss Janes; so I applied bandages on her. Mrs. Browning and the Dr. looking on. The first bandage went round the arm and body. Second fracture we had to splint the arm, and bandage also put in sling. Third bandage was around the elbow, fourth bandage around the fore arm, the last one around the hand."

The VADs had to pay for their own training and they did not receive any wages until 1915, when the British War Office gave them an annual salary of £20. As a result, the VADs typically came from the middle and upper classes; they could afford training fees and had enough time and money to work for little or no income.

By the time Cluett joined the VAD in 1916, there was an urgent need for nurses overseas. Europe's casualty hospitals were chronically understaffed and medical personnel were overwhelmed by the thousands of wounded soldiers who poured in from the front lines. The VAD decided to cut its training program from about seven to four weeks so it could send more VADs overseas. Cluett took her exams on October 24.

"Miss Janes and I went to Dr. Burden's last Tuesday night to be examined on First Aid and Home Nursing," she wrote on October 29, 1916. "The

seed meal poultice, etc. He asked a good many questions. After he told us we passed you can imagine how light we felt."

After the VADs had completed their training in St. John's, they were despatched overseas. Newfoundland and Labrador sent its first contingent of five VADs overseas in November 1915. By the end of the war, about 40 had left the island.

Cluett departed Newfoundland about a year later. After a brief stay in New York and then London, she was assigned to the Fourth Northern General Hospital in Lincoln, England. The facility received convoy after convoy of wounded soldiers from the front lines: young men with gunshot wounds, missing limbs, and other terrible injuries. She spent the first few weeks struggling to adjust to the brutality of war.

Frances Cluett. *ASC, Coll. 174 5.02.006*

both of us passed. He asked us quite a few questions. Miss Janes was supposed to have a broken collar bone and a severe bleeding from the palm of the hand which could not be stopped, I of course had to treat it. He then asked me how I would change an under sheet for a person who was very ill. He then asked me what I would do in a case of diphtheria, what disinfectants I would use, and how strong to use them. I had to read the clinical thermometer, and treat a case of poisoning. He asked me how to make a lin-

"The fifth day when I was helping 'Sister' with the dressings, I fainted away," she wrote to her mother on December 31, 1916. "When I came to myself I was stretched out on the floor. I tell you I have seen some horrible wounds. I often have to turn my head and look out through the window."

Artwork promoting the VAD during the war. *ASC, Coll. 322 1.01, pages 5 and 37*

Pinx. H. TENRÉ. Dévouement. VVE PARIS
Devotedness. 2255.
Г. Тенре. Преданность. I. M. L.

It was a different world from the fishing community of Belleoram where Cluett had spent almost all of her life. At night, she now watched searchlights strobing the sky for German zeppelins that sometimes bombed the area.

VADs and wounded soldiers. *ASC, Coll. 322 1.01, page 11*

"Dear Lil, This afternoon I was on alone," Cluett wrote to her sister on October 3, 1917. "You told me before I left I should never stand the work. I remember hearing you say about staying in the ward with the dead. Ah, Lil, many a bedside have I stood by and watched the last breath; with the rats rushing underneath the bed in groups; and the lights darkened. I do not dwell on some of the horrible and terrible sights I have witnessed."

Medical personnel struggled to treat the convoys of wounded soldiers who poured in from the front lines. The VADs worked long hours and had little time off—one half day each week and one full day off each month. Cluett worked 12-hour shifts in Rouen.

"Night duty is no laughing matter especially if the wards are heavy," she wrote on May 7, 1917. "I have the care of five wards at night; so you can imagine I am kept a bit busy. I sometimes feel very sleepy around the hours of one and two; but sleep must be sacrificed by all accounts, as one must keep a look out for all sorts of things, such as amputation, bleedings, deaths, drinks,

Most of the Newfoundland and Labrador women who volunteered overseas served in Europe's overworked military hospitals. They cleaned wards, sterilized medical equipment, bandaged wounds, bathed patients, prepared their meals, and made their beds. If patients were too wounded to hold a book or pen, the VADs read aloud to them and wrote their letters. They also watched over the dying soldiers and prepared their bodies for the mortuary.

The work took a heavy emotional and physical toll. The VADs cared for injured soldiers, some of whom would never heal.

Sybil Johnson, who left her home in St. John's to serve in a military hospital near Liverpool, described her war experiences in her diary.

"The last few days have been awful," she wrote on September 27, 1917. "Poor old Sergeant MacD, a Nova Scotian soldier, elderly, had his leg off. I was on alone with the head sister when he came back from op and all the next day alone as the

other VAD had her whole day off. He had a horrible dressing and the drum was so tightly packed that it was almost impossible to get the gauze, etc, out with our old blunt lifter.... The sight and sound of his pain was so awful that once, when I went to the bathroom with a tray full of dressings, I found myself panting and had to lean against the wall. Then I remembered that every second of waiting meant pain for him."

Johnson remained in England for the war, but Frances Cluett was transferred to a military hospital in Rouen, France, in April 1917. After only five months in England, she was going to the front lines. The rapid promotion was a testament to her skill, but it was also a symptom of the medical crisis facing Allied forces. At the start of the war, only the most experienced VADs were stationed near the front lines—now, rookies were being shipped off to the overtaxed and understaffed warzone hospitals. But in the chaos of war, everyone had to rise far above their training and fears.

Sybil Johnson and a page from her diary. *ASC, Coll. 201 2.03.02, page 71*

Spring cleaning in a military ward, 1916. *ASC, Coll. 322 1.01, page 13*

VADs serve Christmas dinner, 1916. *ASC, Coll. 322 1.01, page 30*

In caring for men whose bodies and minds had been shattered by war, the sadness was often inescapable. Many of the VADs had relatives fighting in the armed forces—the wounded and dying soldiers in their wards must have been a reminder of the dangers their loved ones faced.

Frances Cluett lost her cousin in the war. Lieutenant Vincent Cluett of the Newfoundland Regiment was 21 years old when he died at the Battle of Cambrai in France on November 26, 1917.

"Last Saturday night I was at Newfoundland headquarters in Rouen, making inquiries about him," she wrote home on December 9, 1917. "Seargent Dewling from St. John's told me that his people would probably hear of his death on Monday night; and did they hear on Monday night, mother. He used to write me such long letters describing everything, and of course I used to write some very funny things to him, but never again.

"The Newfoundland regiment is getting served pretty badly. In the last attack nearly all the officers were killed. While I was talking to Sergeant Dewling, the phone rang, which told him of more deaths of our boys. He says our boys are getting cut up altogether."

Although the work was traumatic, it also gave the VADs and the professional nurses who went overseas a deep sense of satisfaction and accomplishment. They made significant and very public contributions to the war effort. They had also worked within a matriarchal hierarchy, which was rare in the early 20th century.

etc. This is a very wicked world mother; you cannot realize what sufferings there are. Some of the misery will ever live in my memory; it seems to me now as though I shall always have sad sights in my eyes."

It was little different in England, where Sybil Johnson struggled to keep up with her ever-expanding workload:

"We are really like a clearing station. A convoy comes in and is sent out again in two days except a few who are kept for ops. Then we have a fresh lot of names and diets to remember, and the bedmaking and stripping again are incessant. I haven't been outside the grounds excepting a few trips to the village, for ages. Come off duty and lie in my bed and sleep or read. Today I have a great longing on me to run away from ugly sights and the sounds of pain and the constant strain of being responsible for so many things."

Ruby Ayre

Love and Loss

Janet Miller Ayre (left) also lost loved ones during the war. Originally from St. John's, she served as VAD in Scotland, where she married Captain Eric Ayre of the Newfoundland Regiment (right). The union only lasted for about a year. Eric was one of the many soldiers killed in the Battle of Beaumont-Hamel on July 1, 1916. One year later, Janet's brother Andrew died of pneumonia in a London hospital, after spending 16 months in the trenches. Janet stayed overseas until the war ended, and then returned to Newfoundland.

When the war ended, many of the women found it difficult to readjust to the lifestyles that awaited them at home. They were frustrated because their families and communities expected them to return to their domestic roles, but the war had given them a new-found sense of independence and self-reliance. In the coming years, many of the same women who had worked overseas decided to join a new battle at home—to win voting rights for women.

Women on the Home Front

A group of nurses and soldiers at Waterford Hall.
ASC, Coll. 190 4.03.007

Although an ocean separated them from the front lines, nurses in Newfoundland and Labrador played an active role in the war effort by treating returned soldiers and new recruits, in addition to the usual caseload of ill civilians. Similar to their overseas counterparts, there were two kinds of nurses on the home front: professionals and semi-trained volunteers. Almost all were women.

The concept of a professional nurse was new to Newfoundland at the start of the war. In 1899, the St. John's General Hospital made Margaret Rendell its Superintendent of Nursing. She was a graduate of the Johns Hopkins School of Nursing and the first professionally trained nurse to work in Newfoundland. Another step forward came in 1903, when the General Hospital established its own school of nursing under the direction of Mary Southcott, a graduate of the London Hospital.

By the end of the war, the school was enrolling about 10 students each year and had graduated 81 nurses. Many stayed in St. John's, but some moved to Canada, America, or elsewhere for work; 10 are known to have served overseas during the war.

World War I significantly increased the workload for nurses who remained in Newfoundland; this intensified after the summer of 1916, when large numbers of

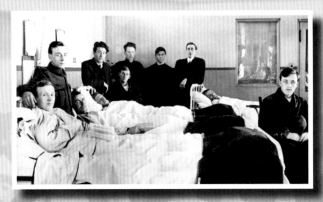

New recruits having pre-enlistment medical exams at the General Hospital, St. John's. *ASC, Coll. 190 4.06.007*

Emma Reid: Home-Front Nurse
Nurses in Newfoundland and Labrador also contributed to the war effort. That was the case with Emma Reid, a graduate of the General Hospital's School of Nursing. Because her application to serve in European military hospitals was rejected on medical grounds, she decided to stay in St. John's to nurse returning soldiers. When a measles epidemic broke out among the Newfoundland Regiment's new recruits in 1916, she also worked long hours to treat them. She later became the head nurse of the Military Infectious Diseases Hospital on Military Road. Reid's work earned her the Royal Red Cross medal, which recognizes exceptional services in military nursing in the United Kingdom and the Commonwealth.

Emma Reid.
ASC, Coll. 177 13.01.009

wounded and ill soldiers began to return home. Making matters worse, a measles epidemic spread among the Newfoundland Regiment's new recruits in 1916 and demanded immediate attention. Tuberculosis was another serious and persistent problem among servicemen.

Recognizing an immediate need for health-care workers, the WPA called upon local women to volunteer. It encouraged single women to join the VAD and serve overseas but implored married and elderly women to volunteer at local hospitals for at least half a day, seven days a week. It suggested that women who had no medical training could take classes with the St. John Ambulance Association.

As well as placing volunteers inside hospitals (both at home and overseas), the WPA worked to equip the buildings with supplies. It partnered with the Red Cross to make ban-

A soldier with his fishing rod and catch, standing on the veranda at Waterford Hall in St. John's. *ASC, Coll. 190 4.03.002*

dages, surgical dressings, swabs, and other medical supplies and to ship them overseas to Europe's crowded military wards.

"Hospital necessaries made here were used in France, Malta, and Egypt, also on hospital ships carry-

ing the wounded from Calais to Southampton and from Alexandria to England," WPA secretary Eleanor MacPherson wrote in her 1916 report. "[A] personal letter to Miss Hewitt from her sister mentioned that she was using some of the Newfoundland dressings in a large military hospital of 500 beds in England, and they all remarked how excellently they were prepared."

Back on the home front, the WPA also helped to establish and run a Naval and Military Convalescent Hospital at Waterford Hall in St. John's. It opened in 1917 and treated more than 350 men during its three-year existence. The association raised significant sums of money to care for the medical needs of returning soldiers and sailors. Among its many fundraising campaigns was the Khaki Guild, which raised money for disabled servicemen.

The WPA also welcomed and entertained Allied troops who arrived on the island. In downtown St. John's, it opened the Soldiers and Sailors Club in 1916, followed by the Caribou Hut in 1917.

Amelia Ruth, cable operator.

Wired Women

As men vacated their jobs to serve overseas, new employment opportunities sprang up for women in Newfoundland. One of the best-paying positions was in the Heart's Content Cable Station. The station had become a hub of global communications in 1866, when the world's first transatlantic telegraph cable connected it to Europe. Not surprisingly, the Anglo-American Telegraph Company was anxious to keep the lines working smoothly during the war and recruited local women to work as cable operators. They earned the same salary as their male counterparts, making them some of the highest paid members of the working class. Cable operators earned between $50 and $100 per month. In comparison, teachers earned about $38 per month, wharf labourers $25, offshore fishers $16, factory workers $14, and domestic servants only $4–$5 per month.

In Praise of the WPA

"The ladies of the WPA certainly have established a record for administrative ability in relation to the running of the hospital at Waterford Hall, and the unselfish service which they have rendered in this connection will not be forgotten by the 350 men who were treated there, nor by the Department of Militia who were so greatly aided by your work. The war has brought out the fact that no more faithful, zealous and effective workers were to be found than the ladies of the various volunteer organizations, who did so much, especially in connection with the nursing of the wounded and sick."

—Deputy Colonial Secretary Arthur Mews in a letter to Mary McKay, Secretary of the WPA, dated September 27, 1920

Newfoundlanders and Labradorians also joined other Allied forces during the war. The greatest concentration joined the Canadian Expeditionary Force (CEF). The CEF fought at many major battles—Ypres in 1915, Somme in 1916, and Vimy Ridge and Passchendaele in 1917.

Of the approximately 630,000 people who joined the CEF between 1914 and 1918, about 3,300 were from Newfoundland and Labrador. As these men were widely dispersed in different units, it is more difficult to track their stories than it is to trace the histories of the Newfoundland Regiment's men.

Many of the Newfoundlanders and Labradorians who joined the CEF were living in Canada when the war broke out. Two early recruits were John (Jack) Hollands and Philip Jensen. Hollands was born at Bonne Bay in 1892, but later moved to Harbour Breton, which was Jensen's hometown. The two became friends and spent three years together as

If at First You Don't Succeed …

Some men were so eager to enlist that, even after being turned down by the Newfoundland Regiment, they tried their luck in Canada. Charles Davis of Witless Bay joined the CEF in the summer of 1915 after the Regiment found him medically unfit for service. Samuel Hackett of St. John's got into the Regiment but was discharged on medical grounds in 1915 after serving in Gallipoli. Determined to return to the front, he joined the CEF in 1916. After the Regiment rejected Norman Fowlow for being underage, the 17-year-old travelled to Nova Scotia and was accepted into the CEF's Engineering and Motor Corps.

A Canadian battalion in a bayonet charge on the Somme, 1916. *Archives of Ontario, C 224-0-0-9-18*

cadets in the Church Lads' Brigade. By the time war broke out, they were living in Montreal, and joined the CEF in September 1914.

The pair was assigned to the same regiment, the 5th Royal Canadian Highlanders. Hollands and Jensen trained together at Valcartier, Quebec, and then at Salisbury Plain in England. In February 1915, they were ordered to the Western Front and were soon thrust into one

of the deadliest battles of the war: the Second Battle of Ypres. They were at Ypres on April 22 when the Germans launched the world's first large-scale poison gas attack, accompanied by a devastating artillery bombardment.

Jensen later described that day in a letter to his brothers: "Just imagine, great shells, tearing up the ground, killing men; besides this there were so many more buried, with

Little Bay's Big War Hero

Two men from Newfoundland won the Victoria Cross during World War I. One was Thomas Ricketts of the Newfoundland Regiment; the other, John Bernard Croak of the CEF.

Croak was born in Little Bay, Notre Dame Bay, on May 18, 1892. Four years later, his family moved to Nova Scotia to find work in the mining industry. Croak joined the CEF in 1915 and served with the 13th Infantry Battalion. He died on August 8, 1918, while capturing an enemy garrison at the Battle of Amiens. His acts of bravery earned him the Victoria Cross.

The London *Gazette* described Croak's actions on September 24, 1918:

"[H]aving become separated from his section he encountered a machine gun nest, which he bombed and silenced, taking the gun and crew prisoners. Shortly afterwards he was severely wounded, but refused to desist.

"Having rejoined his platoon, a very strong point, containing several machine guns, was encountered. Private Croak, however, seeing an opportunity, dashed forward alone and was almost immediately followed by the remainder of the platoon in a brilliant charge. He was the first to arrive at the trench line, into which he led his men, capturing three machine guns and bayonetting or capturing the entire garrison.

"The perseverance and valour of this gallant soldier, who was again severely wounded, and died of his wounds, were an inspiring example to all."

only the boots, or some part of them sticking out of the ground, the stench was unbearable."

Hollands and Jensen survived the first day of the attack and returned to the battlefield the next morning. The Canadians launched a fierce counterattack, but the Germans retaliated with devastating strength. One of their shells struck Hollands, killing him instantly. He was 22.

Private John (Jack) Hollands. Newfoundland Quarterly *15.2 (1915): 2*

Jensen learned of his friend's death later that day. "Well, just as dark, I heard he was killed, and boys, I can't tell you how I felt," he wrote to his brothers. "My officer was by me, and I said: 'I have lost my best chum.'"

Early the next morning, the Canadians were once again under heavy enemy fire. This time, it was Jensen who got hit, taking six shrapnel bullets in his back. "[I]t blew a hole in my greatcoat nearly as big as a plate; it paralyzed me at first, and my wounds looked so bad that several fellows left the part of the trench where I was."

Jensen survived, but his wounds removed him from the front lines altogether. He returned to Newfoundland and embarked on an island-wide lecture tour, telling his war stories to raise money for charity. He eventually collected more than $4,000, much of which was used to open Jensen Camp, a 17-bed hospital in St. John's that treated servicemen suffering from tuberculosis.

Private Philip Jensen. *The Rooms Provincial Archives Division, VA 40-13.3*

During the war, about 300,000 British and Commonwealth soldiers died in the various battles at the Ypres Salient. Of these, about 90,000 have no known graves, including Hollands. His name is listed on the Menin Gate Memorial at Ypres, which commemorates the missing war dead who fell at the Ypres Salient before August 16, 1917.

63

Inside barracks at POW camp in Zossen, Germany. *Library of Congress Prints and Photographs Division, LC-B2- 3384-2 [P&P] LOT 10923*

"We were ragged and dirty and living skeletons, one and all." That is how Private Jack Snow of the Royal Newfoundland Regiment described himself and his fellow POWs in the July 1929 issue of *The Veteran*. Snow spent about 19 months as a POW after the Germans captured him at Monchy-le-Preux on April 14, 1917.

Vast numbers of POWs were captured during the war and accommodating them became a problem. In the first six months alone, more than 1 million people were being held in Europe. By the time peace was restored in 1918, about 8 million servicemen and 2 million civilians had been detained.

About 180 members of the Newfoundland Regiment became POWs and at least 36 died in captivity. There were other POWs from Newfoundland and Labrador too, men who served with the Royal Navy, the RFC, and other Allied forces. Germany opened about 300 POW camps during the war and it was there that most of the Newfoundlanders and Labradorians were sent.

There were four groups of camps: transit, soldier, officer, and reprisal. Transit camps were usually the first place a POW was sent after capture and they helped to move men from the front lines to one of the larger camps in Germany or elsewhere. The men were registered, interrogated, and checked for disease at transit camps.

Non-commissioned officers and other ranks were then sent to soldier camps. These generally consisted of a series of wooden huts, where the men lived, as well as a bathing house and a cookhouse. Barbed-wire fences surrounded the entire compound. Most huts measured about 10 metres by 50 metres and accommodated about 250 men. The general rule: each man had to have 5 cubic metres of breathing space. They slept on cloth sacks filled with straw or wood shavings and were provided with two woollen blankets, a towel, and eating utensils.

According to international law, governments had to serve their POWs food that met the same dietary requirements they set for their own armies. This rule was not always followed and severe hunger was a common complaint among the POWs. Many of the men stole food whenever they could.

"Sometimes we would get a job shifting large bags containing small bags of biscuits like the British iron ration biscuits," Private Snow wrote in 1929. "There was generally 10 men to this party and all would go away armed with four to six of those small bags. We would be searched at the door going out, but nothing to be found. My load was four of those bags attached to my braces by string and hanging down the seat of my pants."

The men were allowed to write two four-page letters each month and weekly postcards. All had to pass through German censors.

International law exempted officers and non-commissioned officers from labour when they became POWs, but enlisted men did not have the right to refuse work. POWs worked in factories and mines, repaired roads and railways, built bridges, collected garbage, worked on farms, and performed a wide range of other tasks. They were paid for their labour in prison camp money, which could be used to buy food and other goods at the camp store. Some men welcomed the work because it provided them with money and a change of scene from the dreary prison camp.

Officer camps were more comfortable than soldier camps. Instead of huts, the men were lodged in army barracks or buildings that the government requisitioned during the war, such as factories, fortresses, hotels, and even castles. They slept on beds and were provided with books and periodicals (as long as they met with censorship regulations). The officers were served better food than the lower ranks, but, unlike the enlisted men and non-commissioned officers in the soldier camps, had to pay for it themselves. Beer and wine were permitted.

Germany also built reprisal camps during the war, which it used to retaliate against or influence Allied actions. Life in a reprisal camp was brutal. The men ate little, worked long hours, and, depending on the location, could be exposed to bitterly cold or blisteringly hot weather. Some were even sent to the front lines to dig trenches or move bodies. Many POWs died in reprisal camps. Some were executed and others simply died from the cold or starvation.

Private Snow, who served in a reprisal camp, described his experience in *The Veteran*:

"Here we were herded in cells about 30 x 10, about 100 men to each cell. This was lighted by one small electric bulb of about 25 watts, and one window in one end. There was nothing to sleep on only the damp stone lavatory. A few boards were later thrown in; a few got one each; but it was poor comfort sleeping on a board of six or eight inches wide.

"Here a letter was read to us from the German Command, acquainting us of what was intended to be done to us. We were stated to be Prisoners of Reprisal and would be treated as such, until the British Government changed their policy of treating German prisoners badly, of which the Germans were supposed to have a lot of evidence.

"Here our rations consisted of coffee in the early a.m., about 7 o'clock. This was made of burnt beans or peas. Then at noon a very thin, watery soup, made by boiling a head of cabbage in perhaps 50 gallons of water and handing it in. No kind of utensils to take it in. This is where our steel helmets took first place as dishes. For supper we had a good meal of nothing at all, which was as good as a change. For several days we got nothing at all only the early coffee, and during our six or seven days there we were allowed out only once, for about an hour. Some were just about able to walk, and had to be helped, they were so weak and hungry."

Snow was eventually sent to a much better camp in the countryside, where he forged a friendship with one of the German guards:

"He had lost a hand at Mons in August, 1914, cut off by an English cavalryman. He called him his best friend, as it let him out of the war for keeps. He was a fairly decent chap. Having taken over command of this section of prisoners in the spring, we received many favours from him during the summer, such as going visiting distant acquaintances, seeing the trains, etc., all Sundays. We used to visit his hotel bar very much, too, buying beer, etc., which was very much against the rules. As it was a country place nobody cared. The German soldiers around here were rather decent, would stand treats for us and tell us about the war and that they were keeping us for keeps, as they were winning. Rather a lot of half friendly joshing, but the bad blood was underneath it, on each side."

POWs in Germany. *Library of Congress Prints and Photographs Division, LC-B2- 3996-8 [P&P]*

Arthur Jesseau
Jesseau was 22 years old when the Germans captured him at Monchy-le-Preux on April 14, 1917. He described his capture, treatment, and escape in his attestation papers:

"In the big German counter-attack we found ourselves surrounded on all sides by the enemy, and they came right in on top of us, and we were taken prisoners. I was wounded in the back at the time.

"We went to Douai for three days, and then to Fort McDonald for 5 days. I can make the same statements about our treatment there as all the other POWs have made. The treatment was very bad. We were then shifted to Marquion just behind the Germans where we had to work for nine weeks in a [reprisal] camp under our own shell fire. We had no blankets or greatcoats and the weather was bitterly cold. We had to drink our daily portion of watery soup out of any kind of a tin can or vessel that we could pick up. We had a small loaf of bread between four men for a day's ration....

"I was sent back to Belgium to a place called Manage for about a month and a half, when I succeeded in escaping from the camp. There were four of us altogether ... We were out for about eight days when we arrived near Mons, between Nouvelles and Mons we hid ourselves in the civilian houses. The Germans at that time were retiring as the result of the big British Push and so we saw the Canadians advancing and we went and met them. They refused at first to allow us through as we were in civilian clothes, and they were on the lookout for spies. However a Canadian Officer took us through and at Battalion Headquarters we established our identity. We finally were sent back via Etaples and Calais and arrived in England on November 22nd."

LETTERS HOME

In World War I, letters were a vital link between the men and women who served overseas and their families at home. Letters brought emotional solace to the soldiers, sailors, and nurses who saw death and suffering first-hand. For them, any news from home was a treasured distraction from the madness of war.

Families and friends in Newfoundland and Labrador also waited anxiously for an envelope from overseas. In a dark time, letters were a source of hope that their loved ones were alive and well.

During the war, tremendous amounts of mail moved between the front lines and the home front. By 1917, Allied forces on the Western Front were receiving up to 12 million letters every week and were sending home about 8 million each week.

Military officials were worried that some of those envelopes might contain sensitive information—secrets that might help the enemy or news of Allied setbacks and losses that could shake morale at home. So they appointed censors to read the mail and delete anything they deemed inappropriate, which might include the names of towns where the troops were stationed or plans for upcoming battles.

Censors erased or blotted out unwanted phrases and they sometimes even tore out sensitive information. On May 7, 1917, VAD Frances Cluett wrote a letter to her mother in Belleoram, Fortune Bay. The censor who checked the letter ripped the word "Rouen" from the page—it was the city where Cluett was stationed in France. However, not all censors were that rigorous and the word Rouen remains intact in some of Cluett's later letters, including one that she wrote on September 13, 1917:

"Dear Mother,

The first part of this letter was posted this afternoon. I did not care to put the whole letter in with the cheque as the letter had to be censored in Rouen instead of the camp; and of course when you are standing by the officer censoring them; you are jolly glad to have just a little bit of writing; it is not the same when we get them censored in our camp; for we just drop the letters in opened into the letter box and know nothing more about them. Good Bye Mother."

In the army, it was usually up to the junior officers to censor the letters that the enlisted men in their units

THOUGH FROM YOUR SIDE I AM AWAY,
MY THOUGHTS ARE WITH YOU NIGHT & DAY;
WITH EYES OF LOVE YOUR FACE I SEE,
AND KNOW THAT YOU ARE TRUE TO ME.

The Rooms Provincial Archives Division, A 58-152

wrote. However, some servicemen were uncomfortable with that arrangement because it meant that a person they worked with every day would read their intimate mail. As a result, the military created other ways to censor information leaving the front lines.

One method was the honour envelope, which required the writer to sign a declaration promising that he or she had not revealed any secret information. Letters in honour envelopes were not opened by the unit's officers, but they could be censored by officials at headquarters or the base.

The field service postcard contained a variety of pre-printed sentences, such as "I am quite well" and "I have been admitted into hospital." Writers simply crossed out the phrases that were not relevant and left in the ones that were. If they added any information, the censors would destroy the postcards.

As the postcards required little censoring, they arrived home quickly, but they were also impersonal. Many people used them as a way to send a fast note to their families in-between longer letters.

NEWFOUNDLAND REGIMENT

A scarcity of news from home was a recurring complaint that many of the men and women who served overseas shared. Wartime mail moved slowly, and it was often difficult to track down those soldiers and sailors who were in active service. Private Frank Lind of the Newfoundland Regiment described the situation to the *Daily News* in a letter dated April 22, 1916:

"Since writing yesterday I have received a lot of letters which have been going all over Egypt, Malta, and England hunting me out, and at last they found me. In one batch I received 68 letters and they've been coming in smaller numbers ever since. It is so good to get letters after such a long wait."

An honour envelope. *ASC, Coll. 324 1.02*

Sailors also had a hard time picking up mail because they often had to go ashore to get it. On March 6, 1915, the *Twillingate Sun* printed a letter from John Luther of the Newfoundland Royal Naval Reserve, which described the problems he encountered while trying to retrieve a package. He was anxious to get the parcel, because it contained a bounty of goods from home: socks, mittens, tobacco, and an assortment of canned foods, like rabbit, salmon, and bakeapples.

"The box is here all right, but they will not deliver it to anyone but the owner. I don't know when I shall be able to get it. You see we are at sea nearly all the time, and when we get in port it is only for coal, and we leave again soon after we are finished coaling, and can't get ashore in the day. We arrived here on the tenth and are leaving here tomorrow. Perhaps next trip we may get an afternoon's leave and then I may get it."

The slowness of the mail also upset people in Newfoundland and Labrador. They hated to imagine the extreme discomforts that their family and friends had to endure overseas and wanted to help by sending frequent letters and gifts. When a package did not arrive on time, it was a reminder of just how helpless people at home were to protect and comfort their loved ones overseas. Among those helpless individuals was Emilie Knight—a mother who was doing her best to make life better for her son in the Newfoundland Regiment.

"My dear Will," she wrote on June 23, 1916. "I was delighted to hear you were quite well again. But I am sorry to hear you had not received the parcels up to the time of writing because I think there was plenty of time. I am sending two pairs of socks now and some Prince Albert tobacco. They use it here now, for making cigarettes."

Gifts like those brought physical comfort and a taste of home to the men and women serving in far-off, war-torn lands. Frances Cluett described her delight at receiving a parcel from her mother, even though not all of its contents survived the trip:

"I got the cake parcel; but sad to say the cakes were mixed together as one and

beaten to pieces just like sawdust. First looking into the box you would really think it was a box of sawdust; but of course it tasted quite differently; I am more than thankful to you mother for sending them; it was a great pity they were smashed! It is very little use sending anything in a cardboard box; it is bound to get broken … I was so glad of the sugar, for one cannot buy an ounce for love or money. I have a tin of cocoa in my room that one of the patients gave me, and almost every night before I go to bed I have a cup of it; but without sweetness; so mother that sugar is like gold to me; one has almost to count the grains before using it."

Even more important than gifts of food and clothing was the emotional support that came with a letter from home. Letters bound together families that had been torn apart by war. They were a lifeline for the people who served overseas—a link to a safe and familiar world to which they longed to return. Writing letters was also therapeutic because it gave the soldiers, sailors, and nurses a way to share their innermost thoughts with the people who cared the most for them.

One hundred years later, the letters of World War I give us valuable insight into the human side of battle. They tell an intimate and immediate story that cannot be recreated by official histories, military records, or government documents. The letters let us see the everyday realities of the war, as it unfolded and through the eyes of people on the ground—soldiers like Frank Lind, sailors like John Luther, nurses like Frances Cluett, and family members like Emilie Knight. The letters put a human face on a sprawling and terrible war that stretched across continents and years, and altered the course of world history.

Just clench your teeth when you read the lists of the wounded and the dead,
And if the names that you love are there—be proud! and hold up your head,
Don't cry! They sleep in the Rest of Heaven! They stand in the Glory of God!

REPORTING THE WAR

The St. John's Daily Star

Newfoundland

| VOLUME III. | ($3.00 per Annum) | MONDAY, SEPTEMBER 10, 1917. | (Price: One Cent.) | No. 207. |

HEAVY FIGHTING AT VERDUN
FRENCH TROOPS VICTORIOUS

NEWFOUNDLAND REGT. WINS FRESH LAURELS IN SUCCESSFUL OPERATION ON THE WEST FRONT

N.F. MEN WIN HIGH PRAISE

Charge Across a Floating Swamp" and Attack and Capture Strong Fortified Positions of the Germans.

FINE EXHIBITION OF DETERMINATION

(Montreal Star Dispatch.)
LONDON, Sept. 4.—Perry Robinson, in a dispatch to the Daily News, tells of the good work of the Newfoundland troops in the advance beyond Steinbeck in Flanders, when they were among troops whose task it was to cross 500 yards of what is known as the "floating swamp" to attack strong fortified positions.

UNCOVERS BOMB FACTORY

Accident Reveals Nest of Huns In Hoboken

Hoboken, N.J., Sept. 9.—What appeared to be a fully equipped bomb-making plant was discovered by the police last night when an explosion blew off the roof of a small building in Third Street as two detectives were passing.

A man who fled from the building was seized by one of the officers. He gave the name of Robert Lichenfeldt and his age as 53 years. He admitted he is of German birth.

Repulse For Huns

Paris, Sept. 8—German attacks last night in Lorraine, east of Rheims, and on the Aisne front, were repulsed, it is announced officially. The French took prisoners in the course of successful raids.

the best they could. Those who were hit badly sank into the ooze. Some, slightly wounded, went after their comrades or made their way back, but the best they could.

MORE VERDUN BATTLES RAGE

Germans Launch Heavy Attacks On Meuse Positions of the French, But Meet With Repulse

BRITISH ATTACK NEAR ST. QUENTIN

NEW YORK, Sept. 9.—Again the French and Germans are engaged in extremely heavy fighting in the Verdun sector, with the Germans trying to recoup their losses of the end of last week on the right bank of the Meuse, but with General Petain's forces holding them back almost everywhere and covering the ground with their dead over a front of nearly

SWEDES PLAY GAME OF HUNS

Swedish Legation in the Argentina Secretly Conveys Messages From and To German Government

SWEDE-U.S. BREAK MAY BE A RESULT

WASHINGTON, Sept. 10.—The Government exposure of the fact that Sweden's Legation in Argentina acted as a secret channel of communication for Count Luxburg, a German charge in Buenos Aires, and between the Foreign Office, has created a sensation which absorbs the diplomats' attention almost to the exclusion of all other

Newspapers also played an important role in the movement of information between the home front and the front lines, although in a much less intimate way than letters. Men and women serving in Europe loved to receive a Newfoundland newspaper in the mail because it connected them to their homeland and gave them a welcome distraction from war. Even the advertisements injected a nostalgic sense of the familiar into the foreign war-torn landscapes they now inhabited.

Back in Newfoundland, people scoured the newspapers every day for information about the war—and there was plenty. War news filled the pages of the local press. Foreign reports were wired from across the ocean, casualty lists were printed almost daily, and local editorials and let-

ters to the editor frequently discussed the war.

Servicemen also wrote to local newspapers from overseas and some, like Frank Lind of the Newfoundland Regiment, wrote so frequently that they served as unofficial war correspondents. Lind sent 32 letters to the *Daily News* during the war, beginning December 26, 1914, in Scotland and ending on June 29, 1916, in France, two days before he was killed at Beaumont-Hamel. His witty and charismatic writing helped to boost morale at home, while keeping an entire dominion informed of the Regiment's actions overseas—although there was usually a delay of about a month between the time his letter was written and its being printed in the paper.

"Just a line or two on the eve of our departure for the Dardanelles," he wrote on August 17, 1915. "The King is coming today to inspect us and wish us God-speed, and we leave tomorrow for Southampton to embark. Today we have all been fitted out with new uniforms, as those we have been using are too warm for out there. We now have been given very thin cotton stuff, khaki colour, and khaki helmets. I can tell you we look some stylish in that rig. No doubt you will be seeing views of us. The helmets are far ahead of the caps we've been wearing, 'perfect dreams,' (ahem!) I expect all the ladies in Newfoundland will be having their hats 'Helmet shape' next season in honour of the Newfoundland battalion."

Lind became so popular back home that even a casual remark about his favourite brand of tobacco sparked an island-wide fundraising campaign. "The hardest problem we (smokers) have to face is the tobacco, it is almost impossible to get good tobacco in this country, a stick of 'Mayo' is indeed a luxury," he wrote from Stobs Camp, Scotland, on May 20, 1915. A few months later, 770 kilograms of Mayo tobacco arrived at the camp. More followed.

Although Lind's letters to the press, and those from other servicemen, gave people in Newfoundland a sense of life overseas, they tended to gloss over the brutality of war. So did most of the content the newspapers printed, which generally strove to keep morale high while supporting the Allied war effort.

As a result, the newspapers only provided a partial and imperfect picture of the war. There were other limitations too. The difficulties of relaying accurate and timely information from the battlefield to the press-

Frank "Mayo" Lind.
Newfoundland Quarterly *17.1 (1917)*

A fourth shipment from the "May-O-Lind Tobacco Fund" to troops overseas. *Heritage Website*

The Daily News, St. John's

Prohibition

CHRISTMAS MAY-O-LINDS

Our Lads In Khaki And Our Boys In Blue

room sometimes led to the publication of false information. An example occurred early in the war, when local newspapers erroneously reported that Britain's Royal Navy had defeated German forces in the North Sea.

"Britannia Still Rules the Waves!" the *Evening Telegram* headlined on August 7, 1914. One day later it announced the victory was nothing but rumour. "Amidst the disappointment it is pleasing to learn that the British Government is organizing a publicity department, which will give out such true and authentic intelligence as may not embarrass the operations of the sea and land forces of ourselves and our allies."

The slowness of communications was another problem, especially for families searching casualty lists for news of their loved ones. It could take weeks for the names of the killed and wounded to be reported, and even then faulty information sometimes crept into the newspapers.

Government censorship laws also restricted what could be printed. In Newfoundland, newspapers were prohibited from publishing any information deemed useful to the enemy, which included the dates that troops were scheduled to sail across the Atlantic, as well as photos of troopships and of submarines in the harbour. Nonetheless, local newspapers sometimes failed to comply with regulations, much to the chagrin of local military officials.

After the *Daily News* reported on the movements of the *Clan MacNaughton* while it was carrying naval reservists in May 1915, Reserve Commander Anthony MacDermott sent the clipping to Newfoundland's Colonial Secretary and Chief Censor John R. Bennett along with a note: "I respectfully request that you will give orders that any newspapers containing any such information be not allowed to pass through the post."

Censors were stricter on the other side of the Atlantic and this limited what Lind and the other servicemen could write to the Newfoundland newspapers.

"Before I begin, let me say that the censorship is very strict, all letters are read over and censored and anything not allowed is erased, so you will understand if every now and again you find a blank, but I shall try to steer clear of saying anything that will give the Censor trouble," Lind wrote to the *Daily News* on April 21, 1916, from "Somewhere in France."

One hundred years later, the wartime newspapers give us invaluable insight into the war and the society that lived through it. On almost every page, war news shares space with local news, as well as public notices and advertisements for all kinds of products—shoes, cod liver oil, and tea. Together, they create a fascinating picture of the time, and of what life was like for the people living at home and serving in Europe.

INTERESTING LETTER FROM CORP. J. A. BARRETT

Dear Sir,—

Yesterday afternoon was observed in Camp as a half-holiday, and there being a garden fete on at Murthly, about six miles distance, a number of our men went thither to participate in the sports. The event was under the auspices of the Red Cross Society, which proved a means of attracting quite a crowd from the surrounding towns. In the various contests in which our men took part, they were awarded first prizes for all, except the one for the log cross-cutting, which honour went to the Canadians.

Madame Tempest, commandant

Logger Correspondent

John A. Barrett of the Newfoundland Forestry Corps wrote about his experiences in the many letters he sent to the *Western Star* newspaper in Newfoundland. On December 19, 1917, he described the warm relationship that existed between the local Scots and the Newfoundland lumbermen:

"A great many visitors continue to come here every week. They find our work very interesting, especially the operations at the mills and the running of logs down the mountain chute. It is all so new to them that they give such descriptive accounts of it to their friends, and then they want to see the novel sights about camp. Up to date there have been sufficient trees felled to make nearly three million feet of lumber."

Much sadder news came on April 17, 1918: "We were shocked on Saturday, 9th inst., when a fatal accident occurred, causing the death of 8460 Pte. Selby Taylor. It was the first fatality among the Forestry Company since enlistment started a year ago. Pte. Taylor was the son of Pleamon Taylor, St. John's, and arrived here with the Draft on 17th February, being posted to 'B' Company. On Saturday he was engaged in the erection of a landing or platform near the upper end of the larger log chute. At intervals during the day logs were being sent down the chute from the top of the hill, and warnings were given everybody working in that vicinity. But, unfortunately, Pte. Taylor and two other men remained too long near the chute, they being very anxious to complete the job they had in hand. One log, more erratic in its movements than others, left the chute about one hundred feet above where the men were working, and before they had time to get to a place of safety it hit Pte. Taylor a terrific blow in the back, causing almost instantaneous death."

PART FOUR

AFTER THE WAR

"On every side were heard expressions of gladness that the agony of four years had passed and that the crowning blessing of peace had come to a strife weary world."

—Evening Telegram, *November 12, 1918*

PEACE DECLARED

On November 11, 1918, Germany signed the Armistice and World War I was finally over. Celebrations broke out all around the world. There was dancing in the streets of Paris, New York, and Sydney. In Toronto, a lone trumpeter roused people from their sleep at 4 a.m. with the happy news of peace.

And in London, Big Ben rang out for the first time since 1914. "Bells burst forth into joyful chimes, maroons were exploded, bands paraded the streets followed by cheering crowds of soldiers and civilians and London generally gave itself up wholeheartedly to rejoicing," the *Daily Mirror* reported on November 12, 1918.

It was little different in Newfoundland and Labrador. "The news of the signing of the armistice was received at Carbonear yesterday morning with every evidence of joy, gratitude and relief," stated the *Evening Telegram* on November 12, 1918.

"Immediately the glad tidings were circulated, bunting was spread to the breeze from shops, stores, houses and vessels in the harbour, the brigantine *Olinda* being resplendent in all the flags and colours of the signal code. At noon the bells of the churches rang out triumphant peals, this being the signal for a general closing of the business premises. A monster procession for the evening was being organized with the music of the town brass bands heading the march. On every side were heard expressions of gladness that the agony of four years had passed and that the crowning blessing of peace had come to a strife weary world."

A float at a peace parade in St. John's, August 5, 1919. *The Rooms Provincial Archives Division, E-42-57*

Our Average Daily Circulation. June, 7,813   Newfoundland   THE WEATHER Probs —Fair and Warm.)

VOLUME V.   ($3.00 per Annum.)   WEDNESDAY, AUGUST 6, 1919.   (PRICE: One Cent.)   No. 174

N. F. L. D. CELEBRATES PEACE

Thousands of people gathered in the streets of St. John's on November 12 to watch two victory parades—one in the morning and another in the evening. Businesses declared a holiday, fireworks lit up the sky, and marching band music filled the air. Many people wore red, white, and blue to honour the Union Jack and the flags of France, America, and other Allied nations.

"[L]ong before 8 p.m., the principal thoroughfares were crowded with a moving multitude of men, women, and children, joyously, almost riotously celebrating the great event," the *St. John's Daily Star* wrote on November 13, 1918.

"Thousands stood on Water Street, ignoring the cold weather, waiting for the demonstration to start and, while the preparations were being made from various parts of the street and different vantage points, there was a continuous display of fireworks. Sky-rockets shot heavenwards incessantly, Greek fire illuminated the streets and some unique modern pyrotechnics displayed attracted the attention of the waiting mass of humanity.

"The procession started to parade the city shortly after 8 o'clock and in it about 150 of the brave 'Blue Puttees' took part with numerous other returned heroes, all more or less showing the honourable scars of the great conflict."

Peace Arch. (1919) Grand Falls. Newfoundland.

A peace arch at Grand Falls to celebrate the first year of the signing of the Armistice. *Heritage Website*

The homecoming arch that welcomed Frances Cluett back to Belleoram, Newfoundland. *ASC, Coll. 174 5.02.020*

Similar celebrations broke out across the dominion, but they were all haunted by a profound sadness. The war had lasted much longer than anyone imagined and it had cost Newfoundland and Labrador terribly—in both dollars and human lives. Families and communities across the dominion were mourning the hundreds of men who had died overseas. The lucky folks who now awaited the return of their loved ones wondered what scars they might bear.

An ocean away in Europe, the long and complicated process of demobilizing hundreds of thousands of troops from around the world was under way. It would take about a year before all of Newfoundland and Lab-rador's servicemen and servicewomen returned to their homes and to the lives that the war had interrupted. The conflict had pulled them out of work, school, and other pursuits, dropping them into a completely foreign and often traumatic environment. What shape would their post-war existence take?

As they crossed the Atlantic to return home, the soldiers, sailors, nurses, and foresters may have felt that a second, much less bridgeable expanse of time and experience now separated them from their former lives. The war had changed the men and women who went overseas, but it had also changed the society and people they were returning to. Reunion would be happy, but it would also be difficult.

POSTWAR SOCIETY

In the weeks and months after the Armistice, Newfoundland and Labrador welcomed its men and women home. It also grieved for the thousands more who would never come back. The war had exacted a terrible cost and the changes to Newfoundland society were profound and far-reaching.

Some of the changes were positive. Many of the men and women who returned from overseas brought with them exciting new ideas and attitudes. They began to challenge social norms and to demand greater equality for underprivileged segments of society.

Women's suffrage gained ground. During the war, thousands of women from Newfoundland and Labrador made substantial contributions to the war effort by working as nurses, volunteering with the WPA, or taking on factory and other work vacated by the men who went overseas. Long before peace was restored, politicians, the press, and the public began to praise women's wartime contributions. Some, like soldier Frank Lind, publicly endorsed suffrage:

"On Saturday I got leave and paid a visit to Edinburgh," he wrote to the *Daily News* on June 17, 1915. "I noticed that since we left they have put women conductors on the cars, so that the men can go to the Front. Same in Glasgow. (Now, who said women should not have the vote?) God bless the women. You ought to see them

ASC, Coll. 158 8.11

in the streets trying to urge young men to join the colours and wishing they were men so they could go."

When the war ended, many of the nurses and WPA leaders joined the suffrage movement. They formed the Women's Franchise League in 1920 and their battle ended in victory five years later when the Newfoundland legislature made it legal for women to vote and run for political office.

There were also calls for greater class equality in postwar Newfoundland. An early focus was on education and making the expensive halls of higher learning more accessible to working-class students. At the time, anyone wishing to pursue higher education had to travel to Canada or elsewhere.

On April 14, 1919, the *Evening Telegram* printed a letter to the editor that called on the government to build a university—a permanent institution that could both commemorate the war dead and bring about far-reaching positive change.

"Today the well-to-do man can send his son abroad and get the benefit of a collegiate or university education, and the son of a fairly well-to-do man can also get some of those advantages which in this field he craves. But the son of the ordinary labouring man or the fisherman has very little chance whatever. This is not as it should be."

On September 15, 1925, Memorial University College opened its doors and students no longer had to leave the dominion for post-secondary education.

Exciting post-war technological advances emerged. A need for warplanes had pushed aviation to new frontiers during hostilities, and those frontiers continued to expand during peacetime. In 1919, there was a race to complete the world's first non-stop transatlantic flight. Newfoundland was identified as the best taking-off point and aviators from across the globe travelled to the island to compete.

The race captured the world's imagination and put the dominion under the spotlight of the international press. At precisely 1:45 p.m. on June 14, 1919, British aviators

THE DAILY NEWS

VOL. 32. $6.00 Per Annum.   ST. JOHN'S, NEWFOUNDLAND, WEDNESDAY, MARCH 10, 1925.   Price Three Cents.   VOL. 56.

Woman Franchise Bill Passes Second Reading Without Dissenting Voice.

John Alcock and Arthur Whitten Brown took off from Lester's Field near St. John's in a Vickers Vimy biplane outfitted with two Rolls-Royce engines. Sixteen hours later, they landed nose-down in a bog at Galway, Ireland. The pair won the cash prize of £10,000.

The dominion continued to play a role in aviation breakthroughs in the coming years. The most famous took place on May 20, 1932, when Amelia Earhart completed the world's first transatlantic solo flight by a woman. She took off from Harbour Grace in a red Lockheed Vega and landed at Northern Ireland 13 and one-half hours later.

Wooden crosses mark the graves of unidentified World War I soldiers. *ASC, Coll. 324 3.01.002*

As long-distance flight became safer, government and industry established regular passenger and mail services. Newfoundland became a western terminus for a commercial transatlantic air service in the 1930s, with airports opening at Botwood and Gander. The once-isolated dominion was becoming a hub of international travel.

In many ways, the postwar years were a time of hope, filled with an idealistic optimism that the world was ushering in a new and progressive era that embraced technological advancements, expanding human rights, and liberal thinking.

But they were also dark and difficult years. Families mourned the hundreds of men who had died overseas. The troops who did return home had to make the arduous transition to everyday life. It was difficult, made even harder by a bureaucratic process that seemed both complicated and uncompassionate.

The Great War Veterans Association (GWVA) accused the government of neglecting the returned soldiers. It said that pensions were far too low and amounted to only about half of what the Canadian government gave its veterans.

Jobs were another problem. An economic downturn set in soon after the war and unemployment became widespread. Some companies rehired all of their workers who had served overseas, but many men had no choice but to once again leave their homes to find work in Canada or the United States.

In 1921, the GWVA estimated that there were about 200 out-of-work veterans in St. John's. It placed most of the blame on the government for not hiring enough soldiers into the civil service. Similar complaints

Alcock and Brown taking off from Lester's Field on June 14, 1919. *MHA, PF-001.1-I03a*

came from the public. On July 15, 1921, the *Evening Telegram* reported that it had received hundreds of angry letters from soldiers and sailors:

"The burden of complaint of the bulk of these writings was the manner in which complainants, and their comrades, had been treated in the matter of positions, and in the receipt of post-war pay. The dissatisfaction over both these matters had not yet been overcome … In the matter of positions, particularly those in the gift of the Government, returned men protest that there has been discrimination against them, and that they have not been treated with that courtesy and fair play to which they are entitled."

A public perception that the government had broken faith with the men it recruited to fight overseas grew. The government had asked them to risk their lives overseas, but then left them largely uncared for at home.

But the government was in no position to increase spending. It had borrowed heavily to finance the Newfoundland Regiment and emerged from the war deeply in debt. It could barely afford to make the interest payments on its war loans, let alone create jobs and increase soldier pensions.

POSTWAR ECONOMY

World War I had long-lasting effects on Newfoundland's economy. In the short-term was prosperity, triggered by wartime spending and a suddenly booming fishery. But that was followed by years of debilitating debt, which resulted in part from the costs of raising and maintaining the Newfoundland Regiment, and then paying soldier pensions. The government's decision to build a multi-million-dollar trans-island railway and its many branch lines exacerbated the situation considerably.

When war broke out on August 4, 1914, Newfoundland's national debt stood at $30.5 million and the cod fishery was struggling in the face of growing competition from Norwegian and French fishers.

But then things quickly changed in Newfoundland's favour. Wartime pressures forced European countries to scale back their fishery, which gave Newfoundland greater access to lucrative markets in Spain, Portugal, Italy, and Greece. Catch rates remained strong throughout the war period and Britain's Royal Navy did its best to safeguard the shipping lanes that allowed exports to flow from Newfoundland to Europe.

Growing wartime demand for fish also drove up prices. Salt fish roughly doubled in value during the war and that of cod oil tripled. Other industries also prospered. The Bell Island mines found an eager customer in Canada, which needed a steady supply of iron ore to manufacture weapons and ammunition, and Britain imported

large quantities of lumber to build wooden frames in its mines.

The annual value of Newfoundland's exports almost tripled during the war, jumping from $13 million in the 1914–1915 fiscal year to $36 million in the 1918–1919 fiscal year. The government reported its first surplus in years in 1916 and continued to do so until hostilities ended.

Jobs became plentiful and wages were high. Wartime inflation drove up the cost of some imports, such as flour and coal, but low unemployment and high wages made this a minor problem. Evidence of the newfound material prosperity was everywhere—growing numbers of door-to-door salesmen visited outport communities, and automobiles became increasingly common on the streets of St. John's.

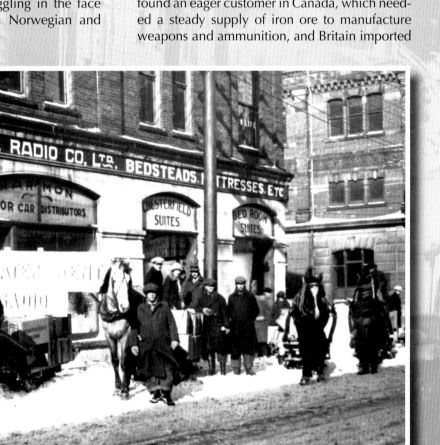

At the corner of Water Street and McBrides Hill, St. John's, ca. 1930. *City of St. John's Archives 01-12-0121*

Members of Nfld. Commission of Govt. Inaugurated Yesterday

HON. W. R. HOWLEY, K.C.   HON. J. C. PUDDESTER   HON. F. C. ALDERDICE   HIS EXCELLENCY GOVERNOR SIR D. MURRAY ANDERSON, K.C.B., C.M.G., M.V.O.   HON. SIR JOHN HOPE SIMPSON. C.I.E.   HON. THOMAS LODGE, C.B.   HON. EVERARD N. R. TRENT

But the war had raised local standards of living to artificially high levels. Many people had grown accustomed to a lifestyle that they would not be able to maintain if trade and industry returned to pre-war levels.

Worse, the dominion's newfound air of affluence also concealed the fact that it was spending far too much on the war and sinking into heavy debt. Much of its spending was devoted to the recruiting, training, and equipping of local troops for service overseas.

By the end of the war, it had enrolled about 6,000 men in the Newfoundland Regiment, 2,000 in the Royal Naval Reserve, and 500 in its overseas Forestry Corps. Maintaining these forces—particularly the Newfoundland Regiment—cost a fortune.

To meet its wartime commitments, the government had to borrow heavily from lenders in New York and London. It accepted $13.4 million in war loans and would eventually have to pay another $5 million in interest. Soldier pensions cost the government another $16 million.

As long as trade and industry flourished, Newfoundland could meet its financial obligations without serious difficulty. But fish prices fell after the war. Newfoundland's major rivals returned to the cod fishery and the markets became quickly glutted. By 1922, cod fetched less than half of what it had in 1918.

Compounding the problem was a global economic recession that had begun in the early 1920s. Foreign currencies dipped in value and international trade slowed. The market for salt fish contracted even further and Newfoundland watched its profits evaporate.

The government reported a deficit in 1921 and more followed in the coming years. It had to borrow heavily to pay down its loans and to provide the most essential of public services. Shrinking profits forced companies to lay off workers.

By the time the worldwide Great Depression broke out in 1929, Newfoundland's public debt had ballooned to $80 million. The war and the building of a trans-island railway accounted for about two-thirds of the debt. Interest payments alone devoured more than 40 per cent of the annual income.

Newfoundland turned to Britain for help. Assistance was offered, but at a tremendous cost. To safeguard its investment, Britain wanted greater political control over Newfoundland and asked that a commission investigate replacing the dominion's elected government with one made up of appointed commissioners.

This happened on February 16, 1934, when a British-appointed Commission of Government replaced Newfoundland's elected government. It remained in power until Confederation with Canada in 1949.

The Spanish Flu

The Spanish influenza pandemic of 1918-19 killed at least 50 million people worldwide, making it one of the largest and most destructive outbreaks of infectious disease in recorded history. Bred in the crowded and filthy trenches of World War I, the disease reached Newfoundland on September 30, 1918, when a steamer carrying three infected crewmen docked at St. John's harbour. By October 20, it had spread to Labrador. Over the next five months, the disease killed more than 600 of the dominion's people.

The effects were most devastating in Labrador, where few medical resources existed to combat the disease and limited communication with the outside world hampered requests for aid. Death rates were particularly high in Okak, which lost 204 of its 263 residents. The frozen ground

Okak, before 1919. *ASC, Coll. 137 22.03.001*

made it impossible for the living to bury their dead, so the survivors had to pile the corpses in vacant houses. Okak had been the largest Inuit settlement on Labrador's coast and one of its most prosperous. By the end of January 1919, survivors had burned all buildings to the ground and moved to Nain, Hopedale, or Hebron.

77

Unveiling the National War Memorial in downtown St. John's, July 1, 1924.
The Rooms Provincial Archives Division, E 14-10

On September 21, 1964, the Newfoundland Command of the Royal Canadian Legion installed a plaque in the institution's Arts and Administration Building: "This university was raised by the people of Newfoundland as a Memorial to the fallen in the Great Wars 1914–1918 and 1939–1945, that in freedom of learning their cause and sacrifice might not be forgotten." Today, Memorial University remains a living memorial to those who served in World Wars I and II. It encompasses dozens of buildings spread across campuses in St. John's, Corner Brook, and Harlow, England.

The Newfoundland government also built a National War Memorial in downtown St. John's. It was funded largely through public donations, in the form of "dollar shares," to the Newfoundland War Memorial Company Unlimited. About 20,000

After World War I, people in Newfoundland and Labrador wanted a way to remember the men and women who had served overseas and to honour the war dead. They decided that a memorial should be built, but its shape was a subject of debate.

Some favoured a statue or sculpture, a beautiful work of art that people could visit to reflect on the terrible cost of war. Others wanted something less traditional. They called upon the government to build a university—a living memorial that would benefit the wider society and bring about far-reaching positive change.

In the end, the Newfoundland government decided to establish both kinds of memorials.

On September 15, 1925, Memorial University College opened. The campus covered nearly 2 acres of land at the intersection of Merrymeeting Road and Parade Street in St. John's. Its single building included an assembly hall, library, lecture rooms, offices, and laboratories for biology, chemistry, and physics. In 1949, the provincial government transformed Memorial University College into a degree-granting institution, and in 1961, the university moved to its current campus on Elizabeth Avenue.

War Memorial at Grand Falls-Windsor.
The Rooms Provincial Archives Division, A 37-56

78

people watched its unveiling on the morning of July 1, 1924—eight years after the Newfoundland Regiment's devastating advance at Beaumont-Hamel.

The memorial is located in the downtown's east end, between Water and Duckworth streets. A bronze statue of a woman stands atop the memorial's central pedestal, representing liberty and the dominion's willingness to serve in World War I. Below her stand four other bronze figures: a sailor of the Newfoundland Royal Naval Reserve, a soldier of the Royal Newfoundland Regiment, a seaman of the Mercantile Marine, and a woodsman of the Newfoundland Forestry Corps.

Sculptors Ferdinand Victor Blundstone and Gilbert Bayes designed the statues and E.J. Parlanti cast them in bronze.

On July 3, 1924, an *Evening Telegram* article reflected the public's widespread approval of the design:

"The monument itself is one of which any city might well feel proud, and it fittingly commemorated the glorious sacrifice made by those Newfoundlanders who laid down their lives for King and Empire in the Great War. In design it is remarkably appropriate, and beauty and grandeur have been combined to make a tout ensemble which is most imposing.... To attempt to do full justice to the Monument in cold print is an utter impossibility. It rests now, an imperishable Memorial to our gallant dead, and a shrine which generations of Newfoundlanders will venerate as a vital reminder of the price which was paid by so many of their compatriots that the world might be made safe from the perils of militarism."

Communities and groups also established smaller memorials across Newfoundland and Labrador to commemorate their dead. Some of the earliest were erected in 1921 at such places as Botwood, Arnold's Cove, Bell Island, Carbonear, Fortune, and Trinity. More followed in the coming years.

One of the more famous was the Fighting Newfoundlander statue, unveiled at Bowring Park in St. John's on September 13, 1922. Captain Basil Gotto sculpted it and he modelled it on Corporal Thomas Pittman, a soldier of the Royal Newfoundland Regiment who had served on the front lines at Beaumont-Hamel.

A second of Gotto's statues installed in the park on July 1, 1928, depicts a caribou, the emblem of the Royal Newfoundland Regiment. Five other caribou statues were made and installed at battlefield parks in France and Belgium.

Capt. Basil Gotto with his caribou sculpture.
The Veteran 1.3 (1921): 34

Moments before the National War Memorial was unveiled.
The Rooms Provincial Archives Division, NA 1527-2

Dozens of other war memorials have been erected across Newfoundland and Labrador to pay tribute to the men and women who served in battle. Every year people gather at these memorials for two public ceremonies. On July 1, Memorial Day commemorates the anniversary of Beaumont-Hamel, and on November 11, Remembrance Day marks the anniversary of the signing of the Armistice, which ended hostilities.

REMEMBERING THE WAR OVERSEAS

Five battlefield parks in Europe commemorate Newfoundland's participation in World War I. Each is built over ground where the Royal Newfoundland Regiment fought. Four of the parks are located in France: at Beaumont-Hamel, Monchy-le-Preux, Masnières, and Gueudecourt. The fifth is at Courtrai, Belgium.

In July 1919, the Newfoundland government made Lieutenant-Colonel Father Thomas Nangle its representative on the Imperial War Graves Commission. Nangle had served as the Royal Newfoundland Regiment's Roman Catholic padre during the war. His new job was to decide on the nature of the dominion's European memorials and oversee their creation.

Nangle reviewed 16 memorial designs and chose one that was submitted by British sculptor Basil Gotto. Gotto wanted to cast five identical caribou statues and install them at locations where the Regiment played a significant role. Nangle favoured the image of a caribou because it was the emblem of the Royal Newfoundland Regiment and an animal of special significance to Newfoundland. He also knew that Gotto's plan was affordable since all of the statues could be cast from the same mould.

Six of Gotto's caribou statues were cast—one for each of the five European battlefield parks and one for Bowring Park in St. John's. The caribous in Europe overlook the

80

Unveiling the Beaumont-Hamel Newfoundland Memorial, June 7, 1925.
The Rooms Provincial Archives Division, NA 3102

battlefields where the Newfoundland Regiment fought and gaze in the same direction that the Regiment's men would have faced their enemy. Landscape architect Rudolph Cochius designed the parks, including the one in St. John's.

The most elaborate overseas memorial is the Newfoundland War Memorial Park at Beaumont-Hamel. Although Newfoundland could not afford to spend large sums of money, Cochius was determined that the Beaumont-Hamel site would be no less impressive than the memorial parks of other British Empire nations.

"The Canadians, the South Africans, the Australians, the New Zealanders are all doing great things in commemorating their Dead and their deeds, and are spending millions in doing so," he wrote for *The Veteran* in 1924. "We will not, however, stand one foot behind any of them and though their millions will only be thousands in this case, Beaumont-Hamel will not stand behind Vimy-Ridge Park or Deville-Wood."

Field-Marshal Earl Douglas Haig officially opened the Beaumont-Hamel Newfoundland Memorial on June 7, 1925. The site, dedicated to the memory of the Newfoundlanders and Labradorians who served during World War I, specifically commemorates those who died and who have no known grave. Its 30 hectares include the Caribou Monument, the battlefield terrain, and three cemeteries.

Beaumont-Hamel is one of the few places where visitors can see the trench lines of a World War I battlefield in a preserved state. The surrounding terrain has also been largely undisturbed,

in accordance with Cochius's plan: "I felt too that the spot should be preserved in its war-time state, with its trenches, its no-man's-land, its dug-outs, as a perpetual reminder for future generations—as a sacred ground."

In 1997, the Beaumont-Hamel Memorial Site became one of only two National Historic Sites of Canada located outside the country. The other is the Canadian National Vimy Ridge Memorial.

Three other Newfoundland memorials exist in France. A bronze caribou at Gueudecourt marks the spot where the Newfoundland Regiment seized the German strongpoint known as Hilt Trench on October 12, 1916. Native Newfoundland plants grow on mounds of earth that surround the statue, and behind it lies a preserved trench line.

At Monchy-le-Preux, the caribou stands atop the ruins of a German concrete strongpoint on the village's eastern edge. It gazes toward Infantry Hill from the spot where nine Newfoundlanders held off a powerful German counterattack on April 14, 1917.

The Masnières Newfoundland Memorial commemorates the Newfoundland Regiment's role in the Battle of Cambrai in November and December 1917 (a role which also helped to earn the Regiment the title of *Royal*). The site is on the Albert-Cambrai road just outside Masnières. At its centre is the bronze caribou, facing the northeast, where enemy forces made their advance.

The Monchy-le-Preux Memorial, 1938.

Newfoundland's fifth overseas memorial, in Courtrai, Belgium, commemorates the Royal Newfoundland Regiment's actions in the 1918 Battle of Courtrai and the Hundred Days Offensive. The caribou resides near the spot where the Regiment crossed the River Lys on October 20, 1918. It was the unit's final advance of the war.

All five sites remain places of pilgrimage for those from Newfoundland and Labrador who wish to honour the Regiment and to remember the men and women who served in World War I and in other battles.

ADDITIONAL CREDITS

Part One: Mobilizing a Dominion
The Rooms Provincial Archives Division, B 3-3; The Rooms Provincial Archives Division, F 52-14; MHA PF-345.022

Chapter 1: On the Eve of War
Background images: ASC, Coll. 137 01.05.002, Coll. 137 04.02.008, Coll. 137 03.01.007; The Rooms Provincial Archives Division, F 52-14
Pre-war Newfoundland and Labrador: MHA, PF-010.001a
Sir Edward Morris: The Rooms Provincial Archives Division, NA 6020
William Coaker: Heritage Website
James Kent: *Newfoundland Quarterly* 3.1 (1903)

Chapter 2: War Declared
Background images: ASC, Coll. 137 01.05.011; City of St. John's Archives, 01-042-001
Recruiting poster: Library of Congress Prints and Photographs Division, POS-WWI-Gt Brit, no. 10 (C size) [P&P]
Governor Sir Walter Davidson: The Rooms Provincial Archives Division, C 3-5 (detail)

Chapter 3: Newfoundland Patriotic Association
Background images: MHA, PF-306.184; The Rooms Provincial Archives Division, F 63-15, VA 40-18.2, NA 2718
William Coaker: ASC, Coll. 009 1.02.014
"European War to Be the Shortest on Record": *Daily News*, August 12, 1914

Chapter 4: Women's Patriotic Association
Background images: The Rooms Provincial Archives Division, B 5-173; ASC, Coll. 190 4.05.002, Coll. 190 4.05.003, Coll. 190 4.05.008
Socks: ASC, Coll. 190 4.05.006

Part Two: Royal Newfoundland Regiment
The Rooms Provincial Archives Division, E 48-60, VA 157-9, B 3-10

Chapter 5: The First Five Hundred
Background images: The Rooms Provincial Archives Division, VA 37-5.3, VA 37-15.1, VA 37-15.2, NA 11029
A ragtag bunch: The Rooms Provincial Archives Division, B 3-5
Proclamation: *Evening Telegram*, August 22, 1914
Pullout: *The Evening Telegram* October 24, 1914

Chapter 6: The Regiment Overseas: United Kingdom
Background images: The Rooms Provincial Archives Division, VA 37-9.3, VA 37-23.4, B 3-12, VA 37-17.4
SS *Florizel*: MHA, PF-008.059
Postcard from Private W.E. Earle
The Rooms Provincial Archives Division, VA 28-171
Pullout: The Rooms Provincial Archives Division, VA 28-171

Chapter 7: Expanding the Regiment
Background images: The Rooms Provincial Archives Division, E 59-1, E 22-41; MHA, PF-345.030

Chapter 8: Gallipoli, 1915
Background images: ASC, Coll. 346 1.01.084; from *The War of the Nations* (New York: New York Times, Co., 1919)

Chapter 9: Cluny Macpherson's Gas Mask
Background images: The Rooms Provincial Archives Division, B 3-2; from *The War of the Nations*
Cluny Macpherson: *The Cadet* 2 (1914)
John Fitzgerald: The Rooms Provincial Archives Division, VA 40-3.3
Pullout: Faculty of Medicine Founders' Archive, COLL-002

Chapter 10: Preparing for Beaumont-Hamel
Background images: The Rooms Provincial Archives Division, F 25-5, F 30-24, NA 1535, F 37-20, B 2-42
Owen Steele: ASC, Coll. 179

Chapter 11, Beaumont-Hamel, July 1, 1916
Background images: The Rooms Provincial Archives Division, B 2-44, NA 6067; from *The War of the Nations*
Five Newfoundlanders killed: The Rooms Provincial Archives Division, VA 36-10
Pullout: ASC, Coll. 158 3.03

Chapter 12: The Home Front Reacts
Background images: The Rooms Provincial Archives Division, VA 36-4.21, VA 36-4.6
Newfoundland Regiment death certificate: The Rooms Provincial Archives Division, MG 956.11
William Knight: from Richard Cramm, *The First Five Hundred* (Albany, NY: C.F. Williams & Son, 1921)
William Knight envelopes: ASC, MF 344 2.12, MF 344 2.13
Harry White letter: The Rooms Provincial Archives Division, MG 592, File 3
Pullout: ASC, MF-344 2.13

Chapter 13: Rebuilding and Return to Duty
Background images: from *The Times History of the War*, Vol. 14 (London: The Times, 1917); *The War of the Nations*
A soldier's uniform: ASC, Coll. 346 1.01.008, 1.01.009
Capt. James Donnelly: The Rooms Provincial Archives Division, VA 40-2.6, VA 157-54
LCpl Chesley Gough: ASC, Coll. 346 1.01.020
LCpl Hardy Frederic Snow: ASC, Coll. 346 1.01.036
The trench system: from *The War of the Nations*

Chapter 14: Monchy-Le-Preux, 1917
Background images: The Rooms Provincial Archives Division, VA 37-7.4, VA-36-29-1, VA 36-29.5
Sable Chief: The Rooms Provincial Archives Division, A 19-26; ASC, Coll. 267 2.01.008
Pullout: ASC, Coll. 346 1.01

Chapter 15: The Battle of Cambrai, 1917
Background images: The Rooms Provincial Archives Division, F 25-15; from *The War of the Nations*

Letter from Mrs. Kate Christopher: The Rooms Provincial Archives Division, GN 19, reel 119, Regt. No. 1783, pages 10, 11 [extract]
Life in the trenches: The Rooms Provincial Archives Division, B 2-37
Pullout: ASC, Coll. 209 2.03

Chapter 16: Developments at Home
Background images: ASC, Coll. 137 01 06 012, Coll. 137 01 06 012; The Rooms Provincial Archives Division, B 3-215, B 17-69, B 3-174

Chapter 17: The Regiment Overseas, 1918
Background images: The Rooms Provincial Archives Division, VA 37-25.1, VA 36-8.8; ASC, Coll. 267 1.04.007
Thomas Ricketts: The Rooms Provincial Archives Division, F-48-18
Warm welcome for our heroes: *St. John's Daily Star*, August 5, 1918
Pullout: ASC, Coll. 324 1.02.005; 1.02.008; 1.03.003

Chapter 18: Demobilizing the Regiment
Background images: The Rooms Provincial Archives Division, VA 36-29.2, ASC, Coll. 267 2.01.009; from *The War of the Nations*
Photo album pages: ASC, Coll. 346
Food at the Front: The Rooms Provincial Archives Division, VA 36.1

Part Three: Other Forces
MHA, PF-319.227, PF-345.025; The Rooms Provincial Archives Division, A 11-165; ASC, Coll. 322 1.01, page 11

Chapter 19: The Newfoundland Royal Naval Reserve
Background images: The Rooms Provincial Archives Division, A 11-165; MHA, PF-345.004, PF-345.022, HMS *Calypso* fonds; ASC, Coll. 041 1.02.013; *Evening Telegram*, November 26, 1900, March 5, 1902, November 1, 1902
HMS *Calypso*: The Rooms Provincial Archives Division, B 17-22

Chapter 20: Newfoundland Reservists Go to War
Background images: The Rooms Provincial Archives Division, F 37-17, F 52-12, A 11-165; MHA, PF-345.025, PF-345.028
Gallipoli landings: Stair A. Gillon, *The Story of the 29th Division, a Record of Gallant Deeds* (London: T. Nelson, 1925)
"Every man-jack of them": Image courtesy of Darrell Hillier

Chapter 21: Newfoundland Reservists on Patrol
Background images: MHA, PF-345.024, PF-345.026; The Rooms Provincial Archives Division, F 37-17, F 52-20, A 2-169

Chapter 22: The Merchant Navy
Background images: MHA, PF-055.2-F32, PF-001.1-A07; from *The War of the Nations*; The Rooms Provincial Archives Division, B 20-137
Defensive measures: Canadian War Museum, 19710261-0343

Chapter 23: Newfoundland Forestry Corps
Background images: MHA, PF-310 3.02.002, PF-310 3.02.004, PF-310 3.01.001, PF-103.3-D11; Heritage Society of Grand Falls-Windsor; *Evening Telegram*, April 7, 1917

Chapter 24: Aviators
Background images: *The Tribune Graphic*, July 15, 1917; Europeana 1914–1918 (Aerial photos contributed by Christoph Herrmann, CC BY-SA 3.0)
Captain Ayre: ASC Coll. 322, page 60; *St. John's Daily Star*, November 3, 1917
John Henry Stanley Green: The Rooms Provincial Archives Division, VA 40-13.4
Newfoundland airplanes: Heritage Website

Chapter 25: Women Overseas: Training
Background images: ASC, Coll. 322 1.01, pages 2, 6, 13, 42, 50, 62
Pullout: ASC, Coll. 322 1.01

Chapter 26: Women Overseas: Service
Background images: ASC, Coll. 322 1.01, pages 3, 6, 8, 13, 14; Coll. 158 8.09
Love and loss: ASC, Coll. 158 8.05
Pullout: ASC, 174 2.03.024

Chapter 27: Women on the Home Front
Background images: ASC, Coll. 190 4.04.004, Coll. 190 4.05.005, Coll. 177 13.01.001; City of St. John's Archives, 1.35.001
Wired women: photo taken by author at the Heart's Content Cable Station

Chapter 28: The Canadian Expeditionary Force
Background images: from *The War of the Nations*
John Bernard Croak: *The Cadet* 6.1 (1919)

Chapter 29: Prisoners of War
Background images: ASC, Coll. 174 5.02.014; Library of Congress Prints and Photographs Division, LC-B2-3996-8 [P&P], LC-B2-3385-7 [P&P] LOT 10923; from *The War of the Nations*
Arthur Jesseau: The Rooms Provincial Archives Division, A-11-140

Chapter 30: Letters Home
Background images: The Rooms Provincial Archives Division, F 37-30, F 46-7, F 37-16; ASC, Coll. 346 1.01.015; Library of Congress Prints and Photographs Division, LC-B2-3460-15 [P&P] LOT 10923
Newfoundland Regiment postcard: ASC, Coll. 209 2.03
Pullout: ASC, Coll. 209 1.02.001

Chapter 31: Reporting the War
Background images: The Rooms Provincial Archives Division, NA 2044; *Daily News*, July 27, 1916; *St. John's Daily Star*, October 16, 1915; *Western Star*, December 24, 1917
Logger correspondent: *Western Star*, October 17, 1917

Part Four: After the War
The Rooms Provincial Archives Division, NA 3106, E 8-29, NA 3474

Chapter 32: Peace Declared
Background images: ASC, Coll. 346 1.01.024; The Rooms Provincial Archives Division, E 42-4, E 48-39

Chapter 33: Postwar Society
Background images: The Rooms Provincial Archives Division, NA 3997, E 41-34; ASC, Coll. 267 2.01.011; MHA PF-345.027

Chapter 34: Postwar Economy
Background images: ASC, Coll. 137 01.04.001, Coll. 137 01.10.002; City of St. John's Archives, 1.12.021; MHA, PF-036.001; *Daily News*, February 17, 1934
Inset photos: City of St. John's Archives, 1.13.021, 1.21.006; ASC, Coll. 137 03.02.011, Coll. 137.02.04.002; MHA, PF-001.1-P34
Pullout: ASC, Coll. 209 6.02

Chapter 35: Remembering the War: at Home
Background images: MHA, PF-315.393, PF-315.268, PF-306.054; The Rooms Provincial Archives Division, NA 2431

Chapter 36: Remembering the War: Overseas
Background images: The Rooms Provincial Archives Division, B 1-87, NA 3101, NA 3102; *The Veteran* 4.1 (1924)

SELECTED BIBLIOGRAPHY

Print

Bassler, Gerhard P. "Enemy Alien Experience in Newfoundland, 1914–1918." *Canadian Ethnic Studies* 20.3 (1988): 42–62.

Cadigan, Sean T. *Death on Two Fronts: National Tragedies and the Fate of Democracy in Newfoundland, 1914–34*. Toronto: Penguin Canada, 2013.

Cluett, Frances, William Rompkey, and Bertram G. Riggs. *Your Daughter, Fanny: The War Letters of Frances Cluett, VAD*. St. John's: Flanker Press, 2006.

Coombs, Heidi. "'Very Able Dusters': The Influence of Class Identity on the Experiences of Two Newfoundland VAD Nurses in the First World War." Unpublished BA (Hons.) essay, Memorial University of Newfoundland, 1998.

Cramm, Richard. *The First Five Hundred*. Portugal Cove-St. Philip's: Boulder Publications, 2015.

Gallishaw, John. *Trenching at Gallipoli: The Personal Narrative of a Newfoundlander with the Ill-Fated Dardanelles Expedition*. New York: The Century Company, 1916.

Frost, C.S. and Edward Roberts. *A Blue Puttee at War: The Memoir of Captain Sydney Frost*. St. John's: Flanker Press, 2014.

Gogos, Frank. *The Royal Newfoundland Regiment in the Great War*. St. John's: Flanker Press, 2015.

Hunter, Mark C. *To Employ and Uplift Them: The Newfoundland Naval Reserve, 1899–1926*. St. John's: ISER Books, 2009.

Lind, Frank. *The Letters of Mayo Lind*. St. John's: Robinson & Co., 1919.

MacDermott, A. "The Royal Newfoundland Naval Reserve." In *The Book of Newfoundland*, edited by J.R. Smallwood, 1:435–446. St. John's: Newfoundland Book Publishers, 1937.

Martin, Chris. "The Right Course, the Best Course, the Only Course: Voluntary Recruitment in the Newfoundland Regiment, 1914–1918." *Newfoundland and Labrador Studies* 24.1 (2009): 55–89.

Newfoundland Quarterly, multiple issues, 1914–1919.

Nicholson, Gerald William Lingen. *The Fighting Newfoundlander: A History of the Royal Newfoundland Regiment*. St. John's: Government of Newfoundland, 1964.

O'Brien, Mike. "Out of a Clear Sky: The Mobilization of the Newfoundland Regiment, 1914–1915." *Newfoundland and Labrador Studies* 22.2 (2007): 401–427.

O'Brien, Patricia. "The Newfoundland Patriotic Association: The Administration of the War Effort, 1914–1918." MA thesis, Memorial University of Newfoundland, 1981.

Parsons, W.D. and Ean Parsons. *The Best Small-Boat Seamen in the Navy:*

The Newfoundland Division, Royal Naval Reserve, 1900–1922. St. John's: DRC Publishing, 2009.

Pilgrim, Earl B. *Freddy Frieda Goes to War: A Labrador Native's Story*. St. John's: DRC Publishing, 2012.

Riggs, Bert. "Reveille (column)." *Newfoundland Quarterly*, multiple issues, 2012-2016.

Sharpe, Christopher A. "The 'Race of Honour': An Analysis of Enlistments and Casualties in the Armed Forces of Newfoundland: 1914–18." *Newfoundland Studies* 4.1 (Spring 1988): 27–55.

Stacey, A.J. and Jean E. Stacey. *Memoirs of a Blue Puttee: The Newfoundland Regiment in World War One*. St. John's: DRC Publishing, 2002.

Steele, Owen W. and David R. Facey-Crowther. *Lieutenant Owen William Steele of the Newfoundland Regiment*. Montreal: McGill-Queen's University Press, 2002.

Veteran, multiple issues, 1920–1949.

Warren, Gale D. "Voluntarism and Patriotism: Newfoundland Women's War Work during the First World War." MA thesis, Memorial University of Newfoundland, 2005.

Archival

Archives and Special Collections, QE II Library, Memorial University
Coll. 158: Janet (Miller) Ayre Murray Collection
Coll. 174: Frances Cluett Collection
Coll. 179: Owen Steele Diary
Coll. 209: Lester Barbour Collection
Coll. 308: Lt. Col. T. Nangle Collection
Coll. 322: Ruby Ayre Collection
Coll. 324: William Benson Fonds
Coll. 346: Charles Sydney Frost Collection
MF-344: William Blackler Knight Papers

Faculty of Medicine Founders' Archive, Memorial University
Coll. 002: Dr. Cluny Macpherson Notebooks

Maritime History Archive, Memorial University
HMS *Calypso* Fonds
PF-345: Newfoundland Sealing Album

The Rooms Provincial Archives Division
GN 2.14: World War I Records
GN 19: Royal Newfoundland Regiment Attestation Papers